Sober is the New Black

By Rachel Black

CONTENTS

Chapter 1 I want wine.

'What would you like to drink?'

The question hangs innocently in the air. What would I like to drink? Around me I can see cocktails being mixed at the bar, I can hear the glug glug of wine being poured at the next table and I watch someone take that first refreshing sip of beer.

I want wine. I want lots of wine. I want it quickly and I want it now while my stomach is empty and it will rapidly reach my bloodstream, quickly course to my brain and fulfill the ever-present need.

Yes, I want wine. I want wine very much, yet at the same time, I don't. Should I or shouldn't I? I want what I cannot have, yet here I am, all grown up, surely I can do as I please? I am torn between the options, exhausted by the mental gymnastics going on inside my head. This small decision of huge magnitude is the first crossroads at the beginning of my journey into the unknown. From today I am adopting an alcohol-free life. I am unsure if I can succeed, but know that failure is not an option.

How can it be so hard not to do something? Just don't do it! It should not be difficult. But it is. So, so difficult. Can I make the short term sacrifice of what I want right now, for what I want most of all? Can I bear the immediate hardship in the hope of a longer term gain? It should be a simple decision but making the correct choice is so hard.

It is 6pm and I am sitting on a beautiful terrace watching the sun set. I am on holiday. I arrived this afternoon at a luxurious all inclusive hotel in the sun. It was an early start and now I am tired and need to sleep but I am also hungry and must eat first. The restaurant opens at 7pm. There was an hour to wait when the waiter asked that simple question.

Today was to be my new start. My 48 hour hangover from the last boozy episode had receded and I felt better. I'd learnt from my mistakes and my many failed attempts at moderation. My hangover mindset had changed from never wanting to drink again to realising that I could not, must not drink again. I had come to the conclusion that becoming completely alcohol-free was the only option for me in the long term. But. I could just have one tonight. In fact, I could just drink tonight then start stopping again tomorrow. Or start stopping after the holiday. What difference would an extra two weeks make? Or would it be easier to stop once back to the routine of work and the hum drum of daily life? Probably not.

In the days prior to this holiday I had felt anxious about the lack of control I would have over my drinking in a resort with plentiful, all inclusive bars: all normal restraints absent, no driving, no work, no pub closing time. I was acutely worried that the bar service would be slow, the drinks would be small and inadequate and I'd feel embarrassed to keep asking for another. I didn't want a hangover in the baking heat the following day yet I wanted an alcoholic drink now. The two were mutually exclusive and I felt panicked by my lack of conviction.

This time was supposed to be different and failure was not an option. This time was supposed to be It, yet here I was hesitating at the first hurdle. Twice previously I had ended my attempts at abstinence when the first hurdle presented itself. A social function, a night out, a birthday, a Friday, whatever. These events were part of life yet seemed like impassable barriers, completely blocking the path and bringing each journey to an end. I know that to succeed I must negotiate a way around these obstacles. I could not afford to fail at the first one. Where would I end up? How much worse would life get? What would it eventually take to make me stop, if not this time?

That evening I was tired and looking forward to a lovely sleep. I stumbled across a couple of thoughts that were to help me a great deal in the face of temptation. I wondered what would be the point of a drink? We were not going to linger over dinner. The evening would be short. What was the point in having one or two? What was the point anyway?

I decided I would not drink that night but promised myself if I really wanted to drink the following night then I could reconsider it then. I would re-visit my decision each time the opportunity to drink presented itself and ask myself, 'What would be the point?', safe in the knowledge that I could always have it the next time.

After the interminable hour with a diet coke we went to the restaurant at seven o'clock. We were seated and I ordered sparkling water. The restaurant was very busy and the waiters were struggling to keep up. Our drinks took a while to arrive and I thought how agitated and angry I would be if I were awaiting my next glass of wine. I observed a man at the next table rapidly draining his small glass of wine and looking around, desperate to catch the eye of a passing waiter to order another. I felt momentarily glad that tonight, that wasn't me. When he succeeded I watched him press a generous tip into the waiter's palm and indicate that the wine should be kept coming. This method seemed to work and I watched him receive and drink six glasses of wine within an hour. I felt a mixture of envy and annoyance that it was not me. I had self imposed this no alcohol rule and felt truly deprived with my sparkling water. The evening seemed incomplete without wine with dinner. We enjoyed our meal but there was no reason to linger and we left. I looked forward to another evening meal tomorrow where I could, if I wished, drink wine.

I had a great sleep that night and awoke the next morning full of vigour, very glad I had not had six glasses of wine the previous night. It was so obvious that I had made the right choice. Now the morning had come I did not regret not drinking the night before. I vowed to remember these thoughts and feelings when sun-down came again.

During a previous flirtation with sobriety, I had some wise counsel. After hearing of all my failed attempts at all sorts of moderation he suggested simply, just stopping. I would then not need to control it, to monitor it, to ration it or to long for the next time it was allowed. What had I to lose from six months of sobriety? Why not try it, just for a while, give it a fair chance and if I didn't like it, go back to my old habits, was his suggestion. "Those habits will still be there, waiting to welcome you back," he said. At this point in time, I gave this strategy some more thought. Instead of viewing every event where I would usually drink as a barrier to going tee-total, I should accept they would occur and let them. I could experience them without alcohol, just to see, however difficult that may be. So every hurdle I approached I reminded myself I had been to these events many times before and drunk alcohol. I'd had many holidays with wine every night. I'd had many drunken nights out. I knew exactly what they were like and they were always the same. Why not try going without? Why not change the record? Why not try it just this once sober and if it is truly awful, return to drinking alcohol at the next one? I gave reckless me a talking to from sensible me. The type I would give to a friend who I could see making the same mistake over and over again, wondering why it kept happening. I knew if something was going to change, something had to change. I needed to try something radically different, just for a while.

The mental safety net of just this once, just for tonight, just for a time, just for just now, kept me calm. I knew I could always change my mind and drink if I wanted to. One day at a time is a cliche but this open door kept me from becoming overwhelmed to the point of panic by the magnitude of 'forever' and helped me get through those very difficult early days. I had no guarantee of what the next day would bring and I had no pressure to commit to it being alcohol free. All I had to think about was choosing not to drink, just for now.

Chapter 2 Then

The pattern of alcohol use and abuse is that of a gradual and relentless increase in the amount consumed over time. Intake may go up and down but the general trend is always upwards. The use becomes abuse and the choice becomes a need. The time and space required to meet the increasing demands of alcohol grow and grow and begin to overshadow all other aspects of life. There need not be a typical rock bottom calamity nor waiting to become a down-and-out type drinker of value cider at 9am on a Monday morning in the park. The action point is different for everyone and occurs when the realisation dawns that by trying and failing to control alcohol, you actually have no control over it at all. Alcohol is the boss and will continue its take over of your life to the detriment of everything else. It becomes the dominating force. Life as you know it becomes increasingly compromised as alcohol takes hold and invades all areas. So strong is its pull that everything else starts to slide, gradually at first but increasing with time until breaking point is reached. Here, life becomes unmanageable and this is the time to recognise that alcohol can no longer stay in your life.

It took me a long time to reach this conclusion. Longer to accept it and even longer to decide to do something about it. Like many, I tried all sorts of rules and restrictions to moderate my intake of alcohol in increasingly desperate attempts to avoid giving it up completely, an option I could not seriously contemplate. My regulations were usually formulated during a hangover and were to allow some alcohol and avoid the need to go completely alcohol free.

The rules started off very rigid and restrictive in theory, drinking only on one weekend a month for example, but became increasingly lax as reality struck. I would think I had set the bar too high to succeed so would revise my allowance up to every weekend. I may throw in a not-in-the-house or not-when-alone rule too. Over short periods of time, as memories of the last awful hangover faded, I would include Thursday nights in the weekend (as Friday is often my day off). Soon, an unfinished bottle of wine from Sunday would be drunk on Monday night. Before long a mid-week restorative drink was allowed back in and soon I would be drinking most nights of the week again. My intake each time would increase. If I had a bottle of wine on a Thursday it seemed natural to have more on a Friday and Saturday. Eventually this behaviour would culminate in another terrible hangover, during which I would invent another set of rules and scare myself with the deal that if I did not stick to the plan THIS time, I would have to go completely alcohol-free.

Eventually I admitted these strategies failed to help. I was no further forward in my quest to control my alcohol intake. I was sick and tired of failing, and failing by making the same mistakes time after time. I resigned myself sadly to the fact that my only remaining option was to become alcohol free in the long term. The next question was when. When would this seismic lifestyle change occur? The answer was vague and always at some indistinct point in the future. It was certainly not Now.

I reached my Now about 18 months before my third and final attempt to stop drinking. It was my first of two failed but significant attempts and arose in part out of necessity. My drinking patterns were changing, my intake increasing and my life unmanageable. My drinking was restricting my life and was no longer a positive experience. I now 'needed' a certain amount each evening (or so I believed). I was no longer relaxing with the first glass. I began to drink earlier, faster. I was finding more and more opportunities to drink and if there were none, I would make them up. I arranged nights out and dinner parties all of which revolved around drinking, on the pretext of 'catching up'. If I was working one night I had to make sure I could drink the night before and the night after to the detriment of all other evening activities which did not involve or permit alcohol. I began to notice my drinking was different from others. I would note my Other Half (OH) having A glass of wine with dinner and being content, whilst I polished off the bottle and looked for more. I noticed a friend be given a glass of wine and continue to chat for half an hour before she took her first sip. Wine had become the focus in my life and I believed I was only happy at times when I was drinking it. Once while arranging a girls night out, a friend added "And we could all have a little drinkie too!!" almost as an afterthought whereas for me it was the whole point of going out.

My first action point arrived after one particular night out. It was late November. A weekday night. A low key catch up with a friend before the Christmas melee began. I had a gin and tonic or two whilst getting ready, unable to bear the anticipation of waiting any longer. Who knew how many units were in each home poured glass? Then down to my friend's house for a quick one before the taxi arrived.

We arrived pleasantly drunk at the small, quiet bistro, and ordered our first bottle of wine. The chat flowed, the vibes were good, the waiters interactive and before we knew it the bottle was finished. But I had a partner in crime and we ordered a second bottle, thinking it was a good idea, while knowing it was a bad idea but hey, we could deal with that tomorrow. Right now, it was a good idea.

Waiting for it to arrive allowed time for my rapid intake over the last 90 minutes to kick home. I suddenly felt very drunk and was once again annoyed with myself that this had happened. It was a small establishment, relatively quiet. I was conspicuous. I was overly familiar with fellow diners. I made obvious, staggering and frequent, trips to the Ladies, claiming an upset stomach. I could no longer focus or converse. I felt so ill and was using all my willpower not to be sick in public.

The evening was cut short and we left very suddenly. I could not drink any more. I had to get out for fresh air. I left my friend to pay, to order a taxi, and to get me into and out of it. I was incapable of doing any of those things. I was truly paralytic, mute, helpless but remained aware enough to feel embarrassed and ashamed. Why did I always end up over doing it, never knowing when enough was enough? Alcohol had failed to enhance the evening, failed to make me happy and had left me with a huge helping of negative feelings and emotions. Drinking alcohol was no longer fun and I couldn't carry on like this.

Admitting it was now a problem to myself was a significant step, but voicing it to another seemed to confirm the reality of it all. I had once heard a recovering alcoholic speak at a conference. He was 60 years old and had been sober for many years. He explained to the audience the depths to which alcohol had taken his life. The havoc it caused. He spoke of the disabling effects that drinking alcohol wreaked upon normal daily activities. I was stunned by his frankness, his humility and his willingness to share such unpleasant events with the audience. He finished by telling us the details of a support group he had set up to help people like us, if we were ever to find ourselves in a similar situation. Perhaps it was just me but there was a real sense of unease in the room, the message was too close to home for many of us I suspect. Now, I dug out that telephone number and after much deliberation (what would I say? where would I start?), I made the call.

It was a good move but very difficult. It made me face up to the severity of my pattern of drinking and I was quickly in tears. This stranger at the end of the line told the truth, without sentiment or platitudes. He never once reassured me that I wasn't that bad or was no worse than anyone else. He never rubbished my concerns that I may have a problem. He calmly listened and made me acknowledge that simply by taking this huge step of phoning, meant there was indeed a problem. He asked probing questions that friends and family would not dare to. Had I ever driven whilst drunk? Had I drunk alcohol while pregnant? Did I drink in the morning? He was not surprised by any of my answers, calmly accepting them as he had with countless others, many times before I'm sure. This was the first time I had faced the facts head on. I recounted my efforts to moderate and my disappointment that none of them worked. His response was to laugh and say 'Well give up totally then'. It sounded so simple yet I knew it was impossible. And anyway, I didn't want to stop. I wanted to normalise my drinking. Even just the thought of stopping completely filled me with horror and fear. A multitude of upcoming events flashed into my mind. Christmas. New Year. A conference I was going to. What about my Friday night bottle of wine? What would I do? No, I was not ready to stop and I knew I would not be able to do it. But I had to try something. I decided I would see how long I could last without any alcohol. I had previously managed without for a ten day stretch whilst dieting like mad for a holiday (although more commonly switched from wine to spirits and low cal mixers at these times). It wasn't an absolute or intended abstinence.

It was mid December when I first started to stop. I counted the days which made me feel proud and sad at the same time. Proud I had gone a week without alcohol but sad that this was such a remarkable achievement. I found my usual drinking start time the hardest and went to great lengths to keep busy and distracted. Just like anything else, not being able to have it makes you want it even more. About this time a new social networking site, www.soberistas.com, had just been launched. a site for people who are concerned about the role of alcohol in their lives and wish to address or change this in some way. I had no experience of social networking and to date do not frequent any other sites, but this one was to become a huge factor in my eventual success. Instead of drinking I could visit the site to recount my difficulties, moan that it wasn't fair, ask for help and advice, ask what others do, or just vent.

Many emotions seem to wake up and want out when the dulling, damping effect of alcohol is removed. I had a million thoughts and emotions all trying to be heard. Under a cloak of relative anonymity afforded by my username, typing these out-pourings became a huge means of pressure relief. They were no longer all bottled up inside. I found I could 'speak' openly and honestly, perhaps like never before, and have several responses in seconds from non judgmental people in similar positions. I read and read all around the site and gradually began to think that maybe I could do this after all.

So, I drove to my few Christmas parties and had soft drinks when a group of friends came round. Each time I felt excited and vaguely high on the party atmosphere and copious amounts of caffeinated soft drinks. I left parties pleased in the knowledge that I hadn't done anything stupid or embarrassing. I was a better hostess and spoke to all my friends without becoming over-bearing. I cleared up when they left without eating all the remaining snacks and nibbles. The mornings after were fantastic. I marvelled at the sheer novelty of having a night out and remaining functional the following day. There was no price to pay. It seemed like a huge reward for the effort afforded and reinforced the notion that alcohol free socialising was possible, perhaps even enjoyable, and was a much better way to live.

I lasted just under three weeks. Nineteen days to be precise. My change of heart came as a bolt from the blue. It is said that people revert to alcohol at times of extreme sadness or immense happiness. For me it was the latter. Between Christmas and New Year I had taken delivery of a new car one morning. I felt so buoyant and happy. We were having good friends round the same afternoon, ones with whom we always have champagne, then wine, then more wine. I had not planned how I was going to break the news that I wouldn't be drinking and I was worried my friends would be disappointed, and feel that I was spoiling the occasion. I was still in a quandary when they arrived. The champagne popped and I suddenly thought 'Yes, I will have some. I want to maximise this buoyant feeling and really enjoy the company of my friends'. I did not want to miss out anything anymore. I had felt like a martyr to the cause at Christmas, trying to prove to myself I did not need booze. And I did not need it, but I thought it would make a good day even better. So the occasion turned out the same way as those times before; champagne and snacks, a nice meal and wine, more wine for the ladies and our friends leaving around eight o'clock. We had all had enough and the event was over. But I couldn't stop. At times like this I would busy myself in the kitchen clearing up, all the while drinking more wine. Once finished I would sit down and 'relax' after all my efforts with yet another well deserved glass of wine, only stopping when I fell asleep.

I tried not to be too hard on myself and my thoughts of the last three weeks changed. I didn't need to be absolutely abstinent. Those people I had chatted with on soberistas.com had got it wrong. They were being overly strict and missing out on good times and even better times by not ever having alcohol. It was unnecessary self deprivation. I stopped logging on to chat or report. That way of life was not for me.

For the rest of the festive holiday period I well and truly let my hair down, making up for lost time.

At the beginning of January I planned to drink alcohol only at special occasions and at some weekends on the rare occasion my OH wanted a glass of wine with dinner. Regular drinking each night would stop and it being Friday would not in itself be deemed a special occasion. For the next year the pattern was wine on Friday and Saturdays. This quickly included Thursdays and Sundays, to round off the weekend. Before long I was convincing myself that a mid week treat on a Wednesday was acceptable and after a Monday I'd need to relax with a glass of wine after 'the first day back'. Very quickly I was back to drinking most evenings. Then the amount I was drinking each night would increase. I once plucked up the courage to ask my OH if he thought I drank too much. He said of course not, it wasn't as if I was downing a bottle of wine a night, was it? Perhaps not, but it wasn't far off.

I took a bottle of wine per night to be the critical amount defining problem drinking and began to restrict myself to 3/4 of a bottle at a time. Or just leaving a little in the bottle. Or finishing it and putting water in the bottle to look as though there was still some left and make a show of pouring it away the next night, preferring a fresh bottle.

More and more to drink would become the norm until again, I revisited the notion of sobriety in my head. I'd toy with it and think it through and always come up with the same answer; that I did not want to stop totally. The deal I made with myself was that if I did not stick to my own rules about when and how much it was permissible to drink, then I would have no option but to become tee-total. My resistance to this option was such that I hoped it would motivate and incentivise me to abide by the restriction and moderation plan.

It didn't.

Time and time again I would bend my rules and end up in the same situation, doing the same things I had sworn I would never do again, and having the same awful feelings, both mentally and physically, the next day. Making the same mistakes over and over again is so demoralising and I was not able to see the futility of doing the same things time after time yet expecting a different outcome. If something's going to change, something has to change.

Not until a full year later did I decide I would change. I would start in January of course. Complete abstinence continued to feel an extreme and unrealistic option doomed to fail so I would be doing the next best thing. Alcohol would be for special occasions only, once per month maximum.

Of course in preparation, I had drunk wine every night over Christmas and New Year. I was left bloated, overly full, fat and tired. I needed a rest, perhaps even a rest from wine I acknowledged. On the 3rd January I identified the 31st January as being the next time I would drink. I would be away overnight due to work, and with colleagues. As always it would be very sociable. I counted the days free from booze and passed my previous nineteen day abstinence record of the year before. Each day was more of a struggle than the one before and it was getting harder instead of easier. My want was building and was becoming increasingly difficult to control. It was as if a pressure was building up inside me with nowhere to go, no means of escape, until one day when it would erupt and I would end up drunk once again. My mindset was entirely of when will this time be up? When can I cave to release and relax? When will this torture be over?

On 26th January after a stressful day of children's birthday parties I felt I absolutely needed a drink and moreover, I deserved one. I hated the fact that it was a need rather than a choice but I was strung out and harassed and it was the only way to cope. Anyway, it was almost the 31st when I had planned to drink anyway so a few days early would not make much difference.

It did.

Apart from having far too much in order to relax that night, a mindset developed whereby I thought there seemed to be no benefit in starting to stop again when I knew it would only be for a couple of days until the next planned day for drinking. I drank every night up to and including the 31st. Afterwards, I had planned not to drink until the end of February, another month away. This was good. It gave me the good run I needed at it, free from obligatory drinking events to make it worthwhile stopping. Sadly I could not recapture the resolve and motivation of January 3rd and I succumbed after only a few days. Frustrated by myself and my continued failure I wondered, what was the point? What to do now? I pushed the thought momentarily to the back of my mind and continued to drink wine.

For the rest of the month I did pretty much what I liked, drank what I wanted when I wanted it (and even at times when I did not really want it). In March three things happened that finally brought things to a head. Firstly, a night out for a celebratory dinner with a group of colleagues. I became overly drunk and made a complete fool of myself. I felt so stupid the next day and cringe even now to remember it such that I cannot bear to write it down. Secondly we had arranged to have some good friends around for dinner towards the end of the month, just before our two week break. It was a Friday public holiday and I was really looking forward to their company and the free flow of wine we always shared. I felt the holiday really began for me a day early, on Thursday night. When I finished work, I relaxed with some wine at home. I had more and more, much more than I intended. Too much in fact, even though it was the holidays. My hangover the next day was the worst imaginable and completely ruined my usual enjoyment of preparing for guests. I just wanted to curl up on the sofa, cancel them, and have everyone leave me alone.

When they first arrived around mid afternoon I could not yet face a glass of wine. Only after a couple of hours and a few salty

24

snacks did I tentatively start on the wine, cautiously at first before quickly gaining momentum. And again, once started I could not stop. I was not enjoying it. I felt as if I was poisoning myself. This had happened more than once lately and I now bought more and more expensive wine, thinking I would enjoy it better, it being of a higher quality. Truth be told I was past any enjoyment. I was stuck in a drinking loop of self destructive necessity and I was powerless to extricate myself.

Subsequently I suffered a cumulative hangover that had built up over the preceding 48 hour period. I accepted then that I was failing at any form of moderation and that I needed to stop drinking completely. Things had changed from my vowing never to drink again to knowing that I could not and should not, ever drink. This time, failure was not an option. The consequences were too terrifying. Complete abstinence was the only way out of this situation. I'd tried and failed at everything else and was fed up with it. I was fed up opening wine almost against my will thinking, 'Here we go again'. I was fed up being unable to do what I wanted. I was fed up making the same mistakes. How could it be so difficult not to do something? Why not just, not do it?

To compound my misery, anxiety and self-loathing the third thing going on was my imminent holiday. I was worried about how I was going to cope. We were going away to the sun the next day on an all inclusive break.

I was worried about the free and freely available alcohol, drinking too much, drinking every day, being able to drink earlier and for longer. Being freed from driving and many of my home responsibilities and their inherent restrictive effect meant I had no means to control my intake and no strategy to cope. Left to chance, it would dominate my holiday and ruin it. I knew I had to stop drinking completely but now was not the time to do it. I had not yet thought about when that right time may be, but for sure, it was not right now.

I logged back into soberistas.com to canvas opinion about what to do on my holiday. It is said that advice is something you ask for when you know the correct answer, but wish you didn't. I wasn't brave enough to decide to stop drinking right before this holiday; holidays and alcohol go hand in hand after all. I think I needed to hear it from someone else, to hear some objectivity. As ever I received several replies within minutes. All of them rational. None of them judgmental. Some suggested ways to moderate; drink on alternate days of the holiday, don't drink before 6pm or after 10pm. Some suggested drinking very mindfully and thinking about exactly what I was getting from it, then plan to give up on returning home. One memorable reply came straight to the point. Stop now. Just stop now. Is it really going to be any easier to stop in two weeks time when combined with the post-holiday gloom and the return of daily stressors in the working week? No. Why spoil the holiday by drinking more than ever? Take the time away as an opportunity for nurturing and pampering yourself. Avoid the toxins of alcohol and come home refreshed and glowing, having conquered the first two weeks of an alcohol-free life.

This seemed a complete anathema to me, at odds with my default thoughts of 'it's 'free' so have as much as possible, I'm on holiday so I deserve it and I'm on holiday so I will have even more,' yet at some level I knew it was right. The seed had been planted and the notion grew and grew, filling my head with all the additional ramifications. Knowing it was right did not make it any easier. In fact, it increased my sense of panic as I knew that was what I had to do. Failing again was not an option. After my false starts, I had to do it this time. I couldn't bear to imagine the alternative. I have had many holidays drinking wine each night. The patterns are always the same and now I wanted to stop but felt unsure if I could do it. I decided I would try one holiday without booze. It was unfortunate that it coincided with this all inclusive trip but there would be others and if it was truly dull and boring I could always revert back to drinking at the next holiday. What did I have to lose?

Chapter 3 The Early Days

The early days were hard. Looking back, the decision to move from drinking to not drinking on that first day was the most difficult step and I bore that in mind each time I felt like giving in. I had to keep in mind that for this time to be different I had to think of it as a positive choice, the start of the way I would now choose to live my life rather than my previous deprived-sounding 'Let's see how many days I can go without until I cave' defeatist attitude.

In the sun the challenges continued.

On the second day I found myself left by the pool, alone. It was late afternoon and my kids and OH (other half) had gone to do an activity elsewhere. We would meet again for dinner in a couple of hours. The pool bar was in close proximity and my instinct was to move over to it straight away. I would then proceed to have as many drinks as seemed socially acceptable until my free time was up. I would then 'act sober' and no-one would know. No-one would be counting. I had to talk sharply to myself. I had to say, 'Come on, get a grip. You can not capitulate this easily to a chance configuration of circumstances'. This was the first of many hurdles around which I had vowed to learn to navigate. This was a crucial moment, a crossroads.

I found a table on the terrace. I ordered a cup of tea and helped myself to two danish pastries from the selection on display. I ate them both whilst reading my book, noting each minute as it passed. Slowly. And it was okay; the snacks were sweet and tasty, my book was interesting and the time was passing. I continued to breathe and concentrate on my book.

Nothing terrible happened and as I walked back to our hotel room I felt a rush of pure joy. I had done it. I had actually done it. I had said no to my desire for alcohol. I had made a change and acted differently and I had done it this time, instead of promising to do it next time. I had avoided drinking alcohol when I could so easily have done so and crucially, it had been okay. I felt elated and bursting with the thought that potentially I could actually do this. This time might actually be different from my other attempts. The empowerment I felt from saying 'no' that one time left me strong for dinner and throughout the rest of the evening. I went to bed having notched up yet another sober day.

A few days later we went on a sight-seeing trip. It was a highly memorable day albeit very long and hot. On the coach heading back to the hotel, the sun was going down and I was looking out of the window reflecting on what a fantastic day it had been. My automatic thought was how a glass of wine would be the perfect way to round off the day. Then I remembered I did not do that anymore. It made me feel sad. Not sad that I could not have the wine, because I could; my new rules allowed me to have it if I really wanted it, either tonight or tomorrow. No, I was saddened by the fact that it had to be this way because I could not ever have 'just one glass' of wine. I have never been able to have just one glass of wine and never would be able to have, just one glass of wine. I was sad that in reality the dreamy notion I entertained would play out in reality with me drinking the first glass quickly and looking for the second while my OH was still only a few sips into his. The second glass would not suffice either and I would be embarrassed to seek a third glass of wine so quickly. However, my desperation for that third drink would out-weigh my embarrassment and whilst getting it, I wondered if my OH was noticing how much I was drinking (I mean notice? How could he miss it?) and what he was really thinking about it.

It was late and there was not much time. Perhaps not enough time to have enough to drink. Bedtime was looming and that would signal the end of drinking time. What would be the point? The following day I imagined how I would feel; hungover, irritable, and impatient with my children. I would be annoyed at myself yet would take it out on everyone else. I would then have another drink mid-afternoon to ease the negativity, smooth over the rough feelings and make myself feel better by blotting out the way I was feeling. I still thought wine was the solution to my problems, not yet understanding that it was the root cause of those problems, that in fact, it was the problem.

These thought processes are mentally exhausting. Playing the movie through to the end like this brought me to the harsh reality that by drinking I would, in fact, ruin this special day rather than make it even better. It was a sad fact to accept tempered only a little by the knowledge that at least now I was doing something about it. I felt deflated by this glimpse of how my life would now be. Reality had bitten and for the first time I sat with this uncomfortable feeling, really feeling it and acknowledging it in the present tense rather than glossing over it, or blotting it out with wine and a vague intention to think about it another time. I felt the discomfort of wanting to drink alcohol yet not doing so. It was a foreign feeling and I was unsure what to do. I felt agitated and panicked by what this meant for the future. Would it always be like this? Was I doomed to be miserable when drinking and miserable when not drinking? Had alcohol made my life miserable whichever way I turned? I felt this unease and worry for the rest of the evening; willing the time to pass and bedtime to arrive, for sleep to come and soothe my overactive brain. It was only due to sheer stubbornness that I did not give in when we arrived back that evening. I had something to prove to myself. The following day, I reflected that I had now achieved four alcohol-free days in a row, despite each day presenting a new challenge. This early success empowered me to carry on in my alcohol-free quest, for at least one more day.

For the rest of the holiday I continued to find the early evening the hardest part; that hiatus between leaving the pool and arriving at dinner which seems to exist purely for having drinks. I took to visiting the hotel gym during that time. I did not want to go and I did not achieve much in the fitness sense but this had not been the intention. The gym was a safe place to be and I thought of it as 'me time' as opposed to exercise time. I walked on the treadmill and listened to my favourite tunes for an hour each time. Exercise is an activity I never associate with drinking and furthermore, it changes my mindset into a healthy positive one and sees me reaching for water. Fueled by endorphins I left the gym without a desire to drink alcohol and with a sense of achievement at another small victory. Once again I had survived the danger zone and could continue to do so for the rest of the evening. Another sober day achieved and my ability to do this thing reinforced.

After two sun-kissed weeks we arrived home. I cannot remember ever having had a holiday without alcohol before. This holiday had been great. So much better than I had anticipated, having usually equated fun with alcohol. I came home truly relaxed and recharged instead of exhausted and gloomy, filled with dread at the thought of returning to normal life and work again. It seems paradoxical that I had to actively keep reminding myself not to drink to keep having the good feelings. Naturally I would tend to make these good feelings even better by adding a glass or two and it seemed strange to think that this would result in the opposite effect. I had enjoyed lots of lovely food without bingeing. I had loads to say. Life seemed sharper and I seemed to have a heightened awareness of my surroundings. I felt different too. I was actively living in each moment that passed. I felt fresh each morning and excited inside for no apparent reason other than that I had discovered the secret to happiness and well being.

The following weekend saw us socialising with relatives. It had been planned for a while, a rare meeting of various arms of my family. Beforehand I had earmarked the weekend as yet another event preventing the start of me stopping drinking. There would be booze a plenty and I could see no way other than to go with the flow, to drink being my default setting. The first time I was asked 'What will you be having?' I confidently requested a soft drink, re-affirming my good intentions. After this first response, the subsequent decisions became much easier. Staying with the flow, on the right path.

It was early afternoon and despite being a grand family reunion I was not alone in saying no to the fizz at that time and doing so was not a big deal. There were several drivers and others with young children. No one batted an eyelid at my not drinking. I had a good time, chatting to those relatives I had not seen for a while. I enjoyed the food mindfully, not stuffing my face with drink-induced munchies. I left, able to drive to the hotel, secure in the knowledge that I was not over the limit, I had not offended anyone, made a fool of myself or been 'acting' drunk. I did not have to worry whether people had noticed how much I was drinking or how drunk they thought I was. I knew I had not been over-bearing, argumentative or self righteous as I often become. I felt as if I had been a good person who could have it all. I had been to the party, had fun, yet was still able to be responsible and look after my family. It was the kind of person I always wished I was, rather than the one who never knew when enough was enough and drank the fun out of everything without a thought for anyone else. A sense of serenity settled around me as I climbed into bed that night having completed the 17th day of my new life.

This type of pattern regularly occurred at social events. The first crossroads, the first decision point of the event was the crucial one. It was the moment where I could be caught off guard and default to my usual 'Yes please' to the celebratory fizz before I knew it, without having a chance to organise my thoughts and activate my good intentions. The key for me was to plan ahead and visualise this moment in advance so to remove the decision making from the heat of the moment. I would consider what soft drink options would be available, plan what I would ask for and imagine myself doing it. I would think ahead about how pleased I would feel if I could conquer another 'first' without alcohol, but knowing that if it was awful I could return to drinking the next time. The first drink seemed to set the pattern. Even after a soft first drink, I relaxed into party mode. Being confident I had made a good decision buoyed me up and made the subsequent choices clearer. It became easier to stick with soft drinks once they were underway. As an evening wore on there become fewer reasons to start drinking alcohol. What would be the point? Would it make things better? Would it make me happier? Would blurring the edges make me enjoy it more? I thought not. And besides, I would be going home soon enough and would be left to deal with the ensuing negativity the following day.

I enjoyed watching the different ways people drank: those who had a symbolic glass to conform to the occasion yet barely touched it; those who drained their glasses and were on the look-out for the next round of top ups; those who looked surprised when offered another, pretending the idea had never crossed their minds, then shrugging with a 'Go on then' attitude as if it did not matter to them either way. I began to feel a slight superiority over those who were drinking. A 'Look at me, I can socialise without alcohol, I'm even doing it right now,' and this sensation would strengthen my resolve that I was doing the right thing.

As I approached my previous all time best of 19 days alcohol free I was not worried. This time the feeling was different. I really was counting up into my new way of living rather than counting down to the next time I would be drinking. Although I still did not (and do not) believe I could do this for the rest of my life, I knew I could do it (and can do it) for the foreseeable future and I tried not to think further ahead than was necessary. As I faced more and more occasions alcohol-free I got better at them and found them manageable, even enjoyable at times. These obstructions which previously had demarcated my periods of sobriety; 'I'll give up until that big work event',' I'll give up until my birthday' are now issues to be addressed rather than sobriety breaking problems. Now I feel I can negotiate my way around such obstacles, planning in advance how I will cope with them alcohol free rather than be defeated by the same old patterns and behaviour.

Some of the benefits from quitting alcohol come along quite early. Sleep is better. It seems more real somehow. Brought on by physical tiredness. Sound and restorative and without need for a 3am glass of water and a 5am toilet trip. I loved going to bed feeling truly sleepy rather than drowsy from drink. Physical wellbeing improved. In the mornings I felt bright, refreshed and optimistic about the day ahead rather than just surviving with that below par feeling from the night before. I stopped wishing the day away until the time to drink again would arrive and I could forget the horrors of the night before. Mentally the changes were subtle. I felt calm. My mood was better and I was less irritable and more patient with others. I felt unusually content. I was no longer pre-occupied by how alcohol would fit or could be fitted into what we did and where we went, and the absence of this constant quandary left me with plenty of headspace for other thoughts and observations. Everything felt simpler all of a sudden. There were fewer decisions to make and they seemed less important. I felt as if I was really living in the moment, as if my life had suddenly been transformed from a hazy blur into high definition.

When I reached four full weeks of being alcohol-free I had what is described as a technicolour day in the sober world. It was the weekend and I woke full of excitement for no particular reason. I buzzed around all morning accomplishing lots of little jobs, many of which had been on my to-do list for a long long time. Suddenly, I COULD be bothered. I WAS in the right mood. I was so productive I felt exhausted by late afternoon. I sat down in my sun room with a ginger beer and lime while the dinner cooked, my son was playing outside in the garden and my daughter was colouring beside me. I could not remember ever feeling this content before. My home-making that day amounted to clearing out cupboards for charity, home cooking to freeze for busy times, making a dessert, doing the washing and co-ordinating a family sit down lunch. I had a little hour of retail therapy to myself in the afternoon and I bought daffodils for the dinner table, chocolate treats for the evening, a few birthday cards, and stalks of rhubarb to make a crumble. The rhubarb was expensive and I decided on the spot to start growing my own. I had never grown anything in my life before but people said it grew like a weed so surely it could not be too difficult? Anyway, I felt invincible at that moment so I headed straight off to the garden centre for seeds, pots, compost and instructions. I headed home, inwardly remarking on how pretty a rainbow looked. Such a cliche I know, but I honestly felt I was noticing these things properly for the first time. I felt so excited about the future. It seemed anything would be possible.

Chapter 4 The Early Days: Help and Support

It was not all plain sailing and there were many times I thought 'to hell with it' and wanted to throw in the towel.

I am a firm believer in asking for help and support in order to achieve your goals. It is okay at the beginning when motivation is high and resolve is strong but as the novelty wears off and the daily grind continues, it is vital to have some coping strategies: people, places, activities to help you when the hard times begin.

I like group support. I think it works. I like having people in the same boat as me going through the same trials and some who have survived those trials and come out the other side. Normal people to whom I can relate, but who do not know me and who will not judge. It can be easier having these discussions with a stranger and the obvious starting point is Alcoholics Anonymous. It had been suggested to me that I go and I had looked into it. Still, I was reluctant. I did not consider myself an alcoholic and I was worried about being labelled as such. Worse still would be being seen by someone I knew, even if they were there for the same reason. I wanted this part of my life to remain distinct from the me that everyone knew. I did not go to AA at this point, although I did go later. At this point I became a regular on Soberistas.com.

At first I had stayed below the radar. Although it seemed slightly voyeuristic I wanted to remain anonymous as I did not want to commit myself fully. I did not want to be held to my private pledge that I was hoping to give up for good. I did not want the pressure to succeed nor the embarrassment should I fail. I was far from confident in my own abilities and wanted no additional stressors.

Now this had changed. I first plucked up the courage to formulate the words describing my alcohol status and to put them down in black and white. The first time someone responded to a discussion I had started I was amazed. Someone had taken the time to read what I had written, to give it some thought and to reply with some constructive comments. I felt as if I had gained a personal mentor. They spoke to me directly, and it was comforting to finally be completely honest about my drinking habits and fears. The replies increased and I received a variety of options and suggestions each time I asked a question. This website became invaluable for providing immediate support and distraction when the wine called and by reading of others' episodes of drunkenness and remorse and their subsequent advice not to do it, my resolve strengthened.

I told my tales, I commented on others', I wrote a blog eagerly awaiting the comments of others identifying with me, finding me an inspiration and congratulating me. The more I put in, the more I got out and the stronger I felt. I love Soberistas and I do not exaggerate when I say it made the difference between me sticking with my decision through the hard times and throwing in the towel.

In reading around the site, I discovered I was not stupid nor woefully lacking in will power when it came to booze. I found out that there were many others just like me; professional women managing a career, a home life, a social life and children, all of whom were drinking regularly and had reached a point where they drank more than they would like. It was reassuringly common to hear of all those others, who also, wanted to drink less, intended to drink less, yet were unable to do so. Despite the best intentions time and again many found themselves drinking to excess and becoming drunk, more and more frequently. I found it was common that intelligent women were unable to learn from these mistakes and several times I read my own story told by others who were also trapped in a ground hog day type of life. They recounted how they would work and cope, drink and relax, awaken with remorse, a hangover and a vow to change, then work and cope, drink and relax....time after time. It was good to feel the familiarity in these stories. It made me feel normal and I was glad to find others in the same predicament as me. It also confirmed that the problem was not just in my head and I was not purely being over dramatic. Indeed, seeking out such websites and hanging around to use them is a fair indication that you probably do need to think seriously about your drinking habits, but here there is no pressure to change and points of view from members at all stages of sobriety and relapse were forth coming.

I became fully engaged with the Soberistas website and valued the opinions of both those sober a long time and those still struggling with the early days. One question that no-one could answer for me was the length of time it would take until I stopped thinking about not drinking. When would I stop wanting it? When would I stop feeling that it was missing? When would it move quietly into the background of my life and just BE, rather than hogging the limelight at the front? When would I no longer need to actively remind myself that I no longer drink?

There is no answer to this question. Everyone is different having their own drinking patterns and drinking history. These, and many other variables affect when this holy grail of calm acceptance and practice of a life without alcohol develops. I was desperate to know the number of days or weeks or months. I wanted a definite time in the future that I could focus on and aim towards, with the knowledge that things would be easier by then.

Eventually I had to put my faith in the fact that it would come one day, and I should be patient and continue as I was doing, until 'it' arrived.

For the record, it first came to me around the five month mark. It was not a defined flick of a switch change that I had, rather a gradual reduction in the number and prominence of thoughts pertaining to alcohol. At five months I first realised it was a Friday night and I had not thought about the fact that I was not having wine. It had not occurred to me. I could now cook in the kitchen without associating it with drinking and by this stage I could enjoy a meal at home and be content with sparkling water (as long as there was dessert). And while this improvement continued to spread into more areas and instances of my life, I still had to stop and consider the arrival of the next big event, be it Christmas or a christening. My train of thought was still defaulting to having a drink on these occasions and I continually needed to remind myself that I no longer did that.

I read a lot too in those early days. I discovered a whole genre of books about alcohol, alcoholism and sobriety and set about informing myself; knowledge being power. There are books devoted to many different aspects of drinking from self help, personal stories and factual information. I found some more helpful than others but common to all was a confirmation that alcohol does not mix well with a proportion of people. While many people enjoy a drink or two there is a group of us for whom one or two is only ever the beginning. Acknowledging that I was in this latter group was a huge step in moving from a mindset of trying to give up alcohol for as long as possible to one where my life would now continue alcohol-free. It was not a personal failing I had, it was the way I had been made, much like having brown hair and blue eyes. It was only after many years of trying and failing to control what I drank, when I drank, how much I drank that I discovered and admitted to myself that it was not possible for me to do so. In fact a person in this group of the population would be as successful at trying to control diarrhoea as they would trying to control their alcohol intake, as I once was told.

There is much encouragement to write in the early days. Writing is therapeutic in itself and provides a contemporaneous record of day to day changes, thoughts and feelings that can be revisited time and time again to remember the difficulties of the early days and remind us how far we have come. This can strengthen our resolve, particularly useful when motivation sags and disillusionment beckons. I felt a great desire to write partly because there was no-one in my real life to whom I was telling the full story and the story wanted to come out! I felt my brain had now broken free from the chronic damping down and restraining effects of chronic alcohol intake and was rebounding with a whole lot of heightened feeling, seeing, and thinking. It had woken up and had a lot to say.

So I wrote lists. A list of embarrassments I had brought upon myself. A list of those who had been on the receiving end of my alcohol induced ugliness. A list of questions I always asked myself the next day. A list of my regrets. A list of events I had ruined by drinking too much. It all came pouring out and the more I wrote down, the more I remembered. My memories seemed to come from further and further in the past. Events I had long forgotten I could now recall and regret. Times I had been drunk and thought nothing of it appeared and I could see the influence alcohol had had on my life for many years.

I made a list with two columns balancing the pros and cons of giving up alcohol. On reflection I was a bit saddened by my list of 'pros' as it showed many unpleasant attributes I adopt when drunk that I need not have again. I was definitely loud, over-bearing and self righteous at times when drunk. I was not interested in anyone else, rather continually talking about my perspective and not really listening to others' points of view. I am surprised and grateful that I still have so many friends. I am not sure I would want to be my friend when I actually look at how I behaved.

Surely they could not all have been too drunk to notice all of the time? It made me a little bit tearful thinking of previous social events although I was pleased that right now, I felt certain that I would never return to those days and those ways.

I was perceived as sociable, chatty, always up for a good night out, always there until the bitter end. I look back and know I am not really like that, I am better one to one in quieter settings. I can only assume I was intent on having lots to drink and extreme and frequent socialising with a like-minded bunch was the way to do it. My 'great personality' purely a side effect. I revisited my lists every time I found the decision not to drink difficult. Remembering these events never failed to shame me. I still cringe reading them today but because they are written down I have a constant reminder that I cannot ever risk adding to that list.I do not want to add to that list. There are so many times I have overdone it I know that if I let my guard down even for just one glass of wine, 'It' will take hold, quickly escalate and the same results will inevitably recur. This is not a chance I can take. I do not want to repeat that struggle of turning day zero into day one. I have changed my refrain from not wanting to drink ever again to knowing that I cannot, must not, will not, drink ever again.

As time passed the memories of these events did not fade; if anything they attained greater prominence in my mind. As I clocked up more and more days free from alcohol, I could see how serious the content of these memories was and the deterrent remained. I had no rose tinted spectacles of a lovely chilled glass of wine on a sunny afternoon in the garden. It was a lie which had been exposed. Any notion to try it was eclipsed by the stark horror of the scene which would develop a few hours later. The script was always the same and the ending predictable. Knowing this did not make it any easier though.

I wrote too about instances when I had been strong and figured a way to cope without alcohol, remembering my feelings before and after these episodes and this reminded me of my small successes along the way.

Around week seven of my sobriety I began to struggle. My emotions were on a roller coaster. I still understood I had an abnormal drinking pattern and knew what would happen if I reverted to it, but I still felt so deprived at times. It was not fair. Why could I not just have the occasional drink? Why me? I had managed a few social events and they had been okay. Okay, but different. Very different. I did not know that I liked this new way of life well enough to fully commit to it.

I was trapped.

I could not go back to how I was but I could not move forwards and fully embrace this way of living alcohol free. It helped me knowing that I had seven weeks under my belt already. This is no mean feat for someone who previously drank most nights of the week, and even more at weekends The perfectionist in me did not want to spoil my achievement to date with a relapse. I was competing with myself, with something inside me to try and do the right thing.

So, I read another book about giving up, and I logged on more to the sober websites, often just to moan and sometimes to read tales from those less fortunate, who had succumbed to booze against their will and spoke of their regret, cautioning others not to do the same. I missed having someone to talk to. I wanted to blurt it all out and talk and talk and talk yet I did not want to admit the full extent of control that alcohol had over me to anyone.

Removing something that has taken up a large part of life is akin to the bereavement process experienced by the death of a loved one. Grief is a multifaceted response to the loss of something or someone to which a bond had developed. The grief reaction is a natural response to this loss and a normal part of healing. The intensity of this reaction to the loss of alcohol from one's life is increased further as feelings and emotions are no longer suppressed by chronic alcohol use. Its removal has the two-fold effect of precipitating a grief reaction and giving the resultant emotions freedom to pour out. Perhaps for the first time in a while, emotions are now visible and their existence must now be acknowledged, addressed and dealt with. It is uncomfortable to sit with these feelings, to wait until they pass with time, when our usual coping method is to flood them with alcohol, blotting them out to avoid the pain. It almost has to get worse like this, before we can get better.

The phases of the grief reaction are denial, anger, bargaining, depression and acceptance. They do not happen in isolation nor necessarily in this order but I recognise elements of them all in my relationship with alcohol. I was in denial about the true extent and dangers of my drinking for a long time. I was angry and depressed that I could not drink. I did not personally go through any bargaining pleas but know people who wish they could have had a few more years of drinking before crunch time arrived. I was beginning to accept the way it had to be for me from then on, but I was far from happy about it.

I planned to give it three months and then review my aims. By three months of alcohol abstinence all the benefits should have kicked in and life should be as good as it is going to get.

It was around now, at the seven or eight week mark, that I decided to reconsider Alcoholics Anonymous. If I was going to continue to live free from alcohol I needed some outlet for this huge change in my life. I needed coping mechanisms and a network of support to help me when I could not help myself. I needed to talk to people who knew what I was talking about, who would understand without judgement or dismissal. I did not yet have a sober friend and I did not yet have faith in my own ability to keep myself alcohol free through thick and thin. I decided I would give AA a try.

Chapter 5 Are You a Friend of Bill?

My previous reasons for avoiding AA were still valid so I searched for a meeting far from my home in the hope that I would not see, nor be seen, by anyone I knew. Although I knew that everyone would be there for the same reason I still wanted to retain my anonymity and keep my 'real' life private.

On the day, I scouted out the meeting venue and parked nearby half an hour before the start. I had a good view of the door and was able to see the comings and goings at the entrance. There were a few people hanging around outside with large steaming cups of tea and cigarettes. My initial impression was how happy they all looked. They were laughing and looked as if they were having a good time. People who joined them also looked happy and pleased to see each other. There were friendly greetings all around and they conveyed a sense of true camaraderie. I had expected them all to look miserable, to be miserable, the way I was feeling right now but nothing could be further from the truth. Surely they could not all be wrong? Surely they could not all be pretending or be the exceptions to prove the rule? Perhaps it was possible to be happy and enjoy life without alcohol?

I felt brave yet very nervous as I walked into the building, trying to look confident as if I knew where I was going. A woman ahead of me hung back and said, 'Are you a friend of Bill's?'

'No,' I said, thinking she had mistaken me for someone else. "I'm here for the AA meeting".

I soon found out that being a friend of Bill is a code phrase that AA fellows use to identify each other. Bill or Bill W, refers to the original founder of the Alcoholics Anonymous fellowship, William Wilson. This was news to me, as was much of what took place over the next hour and a half. My second impression of the meeting was that I have NEVER before walked into a new club alone and not knowing anyone, yet have people spontaneously approach me, welcome me and introduce themselves. This just does not happen at a running club or a gym class. Here, people seemed genuinely welcoming and I really was touched, if a bit overwhelmed. I was ushered in, given a large cup of tea and offered biscuits. A regular immediately took me under her wing, sat beside me and told me what would happen. I became the 'newcomer' My third impression was that there seemed few barriers. Usual social groupings and barriers did not apply here. Looking around the room alcohol was the only common factor. There was a vast array of age groups, ethnicity, clothes, hairstyles (or not), accents, piercings and personalities. None of these seemed to matter. The meeting opened with some AA formalities and then someone shared their story with the group and became the Chairperson for the rest of the meeting. My guide was almost apologetic that the 'share' may not be one that I could readily identify with but that I should try a few meetings as they were all different. During the share I felt wonder at the speaker telling of his deepest darkest moments to a roomful of people and also privileged that I had been invited in and allowed to listen, despite being an unknown.

After a break for more tea, biscuits (a cigarette if needed) and camaraderie it was time for the second half. Here, the Chair would go around the room, inviting people to comment or respond to his shared story or indeed just to speak. I was reassured by my guide I did not need to speak and could opt to pass when it came to my turn. As talking aloud was one of my reasons for going I decided I would speak. I said I had accepted the fact that I could not moderate or control my drinking and was not sure I could remain alcohol free alone. Out of the blue I became over-whelmed with emotion and began to cry. Tears were pouring down my face as I randomly spoke of all the things in my mind but strangely, I did not seem to care. I continued to speak whilst sobbing and hiccoughing throughout. It was such a relief to speak out loud to an understanding unknown audience. I felt a weight lifting from my shoulders as I finally admitted it aloud. By confessing I could really wipe the slate clean and live differently. I felt calm and relieved. Things were actually going to be okay.

Afterwards, another woman gave me her mobile number and said to call anytime. I chatted to her for a few minutes outside and she suggested if time allowed that we continue our chat at the coffee shop across the road. I surprised myself by accepting the invitation there and then. Now that my pressure relief valve had opened I wanted to continue to talk. I enjoyed the hour we spent talking about alcoholism, her experiences and my hopes and fears.

I left feeling a great release of tension. I felt lighter. I could now talk openly and honestly to a friend about my problem and the millions of thoughts buzzing around my brain.

Subsequently I went to a few other meetings. I became accustomed to meeting and greeting strangers with infectious enthusiasm. The tales I heard were varied. People who had lost everything, their job, their spouse, their children. their self respect. People who were grateful for things now back in their life because they were sober, being allowed contact with grandchildren or once again being invited to family celebrations. These accounts re-enforced my view that if I returned to drinking I would end up further down that same slippery slope. No one was immune. The disease, as those in AA believe it to be, is progressive. Over time alcohol consumption continually increases. Our need becomes greater and our requirements increase as our bodies become ever more efficient at handling the drug. More and more is required to attain the same mind altered state as time goes by and more is required to normalise the habitual drinker and render him or her functional. I had experienced this throughout the preceding ten years of my life and felt thankful I had recognised this increase and drawn a halt to it, before I lost the big things in life that were important to me. I always left AA meetings with renewed conviction to remaining free from alcohol. My feeling it was the right thing to do was affirmed and the stories I heard sent me a frightening warning of what could happen, if I were to give alcohol a way back in.

I never joined a particular group or attended any one meeting regularly. Subconsciously I did not want to be one of them or commit fully to their program. Hence I was always identified as the Newcomer at meetings. This was welcoming at first and I appreciated the good wishes and accepted the congratulations for having taken the brave step of attending. With time it became tiresome. I felt conspicuous. Most people, when speaking, referred to the new person in the room with some advice or comment and I felt all heads turn to face me each time. It was too much attention, well meant but over bearing. Neither was I sure I agreed with some of the underpinning philosophies. I don't believe in higher powers. Personally, I don't believe I have a disease for which there is no cure. I don't have a constant day in day out hankering for alcohol and am not worried I could be drawn to drink at any minute of any day. Indeed I still have a lot of alcohol in the house which would be against the advice of many. I have removed my temptations though, and as long as there is no white wine chilling in the fridge I know I will be okay. I believe simply that I have a choice whether to drink or not and that the correct choice is hard to make at certain times. This will always be the case for me and I will need to be continually on my guard to identify and plan for when such situations arise.

There are many sound bites regularly repeated in AA circles and many of them I find very helpful and so true. You never regret not having another drink. You never regret not drinking. Avoid the first drink and you will be okay. One day at a time.

One day at a time is an interesting concept. It is used in AA to keep things in the current moment. Not to plan or commit to the future. It is used to convey a knowledge that while one is sober today, it is not guaranteed you will be so tomorrow. I like the idea of one day at a time. I like that it is a small manageable chunk of time, but I find it has many negative connotations in AA. It is used to depict a life where today is yet another that I'm struggling through. I am trying hard not to drink at each and every moment of the day and it is such an uphill struggle I do not know if I can manage it tomorrow as well. Who knows what may happen then? There is a reluctance to look forward to a more enjoyable life as well as a guarded reticence to looking back, celebrating that already achieved.

I prefer to reframe this thought so as to mean that I'm enjoying this way of life, one day at a time. The number of days passing is not the focus of my life, rather they represent a marker of the beginning of this new way to live. The time passed is an accumulation of many single days of this way of life, rather than a millstone around my neck. I would be similarly depressed if each day I dwelt on my mortgage, another long term project. Despite paying it off one day at a time from now to eternity it does not burden me on a daily basis. I think of it as something I have committed to do in the long term, that occurs from the accumulation of regular payments in the short term. Much the same as I feel about remaining free from alcohol.

Chapter 6 Then and Now: Socialising

The early days continued and by two months I had some experience of socialising without drinking alcohol.

I used a variety of reasons and excuses for not drinking. Usually it was driving or working early the next day. Sometimes I said I'd had too much the night before and needed a night off to recover. Other times I said I was kick starting a diet or trying a new health plan. What I said changed depending on the person asking, and the state of my mind and resolve. I was too scared to say 'Because I don't drink anymore'. That was too big a statement to make at this time. It would put me under pressure to succeed and be stressful. It would lead to a whole host of further questions. I would feel foolish if I did not manage in the long term and subsequently I would have to explain why I was drinking again.

It was not until much later that I became confident of my ability to keep my life in this lovely state of order and only then did I begin to mention casually to a few close friends that I had stopped drinking and would not return to it. Each time I cautiously dipped my toe in the water this way, I was nervous and anxious as I waited to hear their responses. I did not reach this stage for several months though, by which time I was able to deal with any response and cared less and less if the truth became apparent. In the meantime though, my social life continued and I recycled my excuses.

I had previously been invited to my neighbourhood book club and, at nine weeks into my sober journey I had read the book and was able to make it to the evening of discussion.

I had been told the host buys pizza. We each take a bottle of wine and arrive at 8pm. I know the girls only a little except for one, who is a close friend and knows me well. I had a great evening and was struck by how different it would have been had I been my usual 'sociable' alcohol drinking self.

Then

I would lament at late start to the evening so would have wine at home beforehand, probably starting at six o'clock. My husband would be due to arrive home at seven o'clock so I would be orchestrating how the bottle looked; either being not more than half empty or small bottles already discarded. I would be irritated that he arrived home earlier than planned and interrupted my quality, quiet, private time with wine. I would go to book club taking more wine with me and would drink as much as a) the others or b) as much as was possible given the social setting, whichever was more. I would become over chatty, too loud, overeat from the array of pizza, crisps, cup cakes and biscuits displayed and I would stay as late as possible. Once home I would have a cup of tea and a massive bowl of cereal while replaying bits of the evening's conversation in my head. I would wonder what they thought of me. I would drink a large glass of water before going to bed. I would be up to the bathroom in the night and hungover the next morning whilst worrying whether I had become obnoxious or made a bad impression.

Now

The reality was I took time getting ready then had a (soft) drink with my husband while he ate dinner. I took with me some elderflower and pomegranate fizz and a box of chocolates for the host. I declined the first gin fizz cocktail offered as I was 'working early tomorrow'. This was indeed the case but I saw the look of surprise on my friend's face. She knew this would not stop me drinking the evening before, in fact, it may make it even more likely. I avoided making eye contact with her and was pleased to see a heavily pregnant girl there, who was also not drinking. I enjoyed the sweet sugary soft drinks that I would never before have dreamt of wasting calories on. I ate the food, normally, and really enjoyed it. I enjoyed the chat (including the small amount about the book) and I listened. I enjoyed really listening. I never listen very much when drunk; my time is spent talking and waiting to talk again.

I watched the others drink their gin fizz and start on the white wine. No one really overdid it and I know I would have wanted more wine than they had. I would certainly have drunk more quickly. Most had a couple of glasses of wine and later we all had tea with cakes. Usually I am disappointed when tea and coffee is offered at the end of the evening. It signals that home time is looming but more immediately, puts an end to wine drinking. I was not envious of those drinking wine. I had wondered if I would feel 'poor me' being unable to have even one or two glasses now and then. But I did not. I knew it would never stop at one or two and I felt calm in that knowledge and accepting of my decision. I honestly do not think wine would have made the evening any better than it was.

I had a great night and enjoyed the company. I made my excuses at midnight and was the first to leave. I walked home and went straight to bed. The next morning was so different: although tired I was fresh as a daisy, happy to have enjoyed a few treats the previous evening while sparing my diet a late night binge. I had enjoyed getting to know the other girls better and knew I had not embarrassed myself or made a bad impression.

My social life involves dinners in restaurants and hotels with work colleagues. As in many professions, there is a work hard play even harder mentality. Often there is free booze at these evenings and there is always excessive boozing. There is safety in numbers. Extreme behaviour can seem unremarkable and acceptable when everyone is doing it together. Drinking is no exception. Drinking a lot, drinking all night, late into the night, was the norm for these evenings and I was right up there with them all the way.

My approach to these nights has changed. I no longer move heaven and earth in my home life to get along to each and every one. I go to those I want to and to those I am expected to attend. I no longer spend fifty pounds each time on taxis.

Then

I would phone around trying to find someone driving who could give me a lift. Failing this I would get a taxi, at significant expense due to where I live. I would have a drink while I got ready at home and have my taxi arrive promptly to get to the venue early. I made sure I had plenty of cash in my purse for buying drinks. I would have a drink at the bar on arrival and when we sat down at our table I would position myself close to the wine. I could be relied upon to top up glasses regularly and to order further bottles of wine whenever there was danger of it running out. I never chose anything to eat from the menu that I really wanted. I limited myself to the smallest, lowest calorie options to compensate for all the calorific wine. I never had dessert but would be disinhibited enough by this stage to 'try' a spoonful from the plates of those seated next to me. After dinner I would prolong the night with a trip to a club or, if away from home, back to the hotel bar. I would spend a lot of cash. I used to think I was the heart and soul of the party. Now I realise I was simply drunk, and wanted to keep drinking.

I would have slight trepidation about getting myself home alone in a taxi with all bits intact and remaining under voluntary control. At home I would munch my way through a mountain of snacks as by then I was hungry, having eaten very little dinner.

The next day I would worry I had been too drunk, indiscreet, inappropriate or embarrassing. Had my frequent arrogant monopolising of the conversation occurred? Had people noticed? Was I any more drunk than the others? I would also be fit for nothing the following day and would have planned for this in advance by either booking the day off work or making sure I had nothing scheduled too early or that would be too taxing. I thought of it as a wipe out day, one that never existed rather than dwell on the time squandered. I felt awful on these days, physically and emotionally. It came out as anger and irritation at everything around me and I could not wait for time to pass, for these days to be over and the feelings to subside.

Now

I drive to the restaurant and arrive close to the meal time. I relax after my first drink of sparkling water. I choose the food I want and enjoy it immensely. I have a full dessert and savour it. At the table I note the drinking patterns of others, out of interest. There are a few intent on maximising their share of the wine but there are others who drink minimally, in a restrained manner and declare they have had enough after a glass or two. I talk to those I enjoy conversing with. I have realised there are many people I don't actually have much to say to, now I'm sober. This surprises me as I would have said they were great friends, friends with whom I had spent many a night laughing and drinking, putting the world to rights. We probably all spoke a lot of drunken nonsense on those occasions and were bound together only as like-minded individuals who wanted to keep drinking. I no longer want to socialise with this group as it seems pointless. I get annoyed by the drunken repetition of tales, by the statements of great love and friendship, by the smell of their breath. It seems pointless to tell them anything interesting when they do not listen, will not remember and cannot converse meaningfully. As the evening draws to a close I observe a colleague asking everyone, anyone really, to move onto a late night bar with him. As more and more decline the offer I feel pity for him as he continues to invite someone else and someone else. They need not be friends, he just needs a drinking buddy. Previously I would have been his partner in crime.

I am careful about offering lifts home now too. I used to feel pleased I could do this for friends but too often I have spent too long going far out of my way in a car filled with wine fumes and slurred chatter. I learned quickly to restrict my offers or leave a bit earlier.

The first few times I went to a dinner or formal occasion sober I did not particularly enjoy the evenings. I felt a bit empty, a bit awkward. The conversation felt harder work. The venues always felt noisy and talking was an effort. Between conversations, standing alone cradling a glass of fizzy water seemed much more conspicuous than with a glass of wine. I was beginning to think this was going to be the down side of not drinking. That this kind of evening was going to remain less fun and less enjoyable. I could accept this. It was a small price to pay for all the other areas of life which had improved immensely. However, there was no need to worry. Those first nights out were not enjoyable due to the company.I now enjoy these times. They are significantly different for me since I stopped drinking and I know the elements which I enjoy are different too.

I have subsequently had occasions where I have had a fabulous time. I have sat next to friends, to raconteurs, to those I admire and to those in whose conversation I have a genuine interest. I have sat next to pregnant ladies and fellow drivers and each time I have really enjoyed the night. The realisation that a 'good' night out is determined by the company and not the amount of alcohol consumed, was a big one. It has made me think more about which parties I go to. A drinks reception will only be as good as the reason for the celebration, not by the number of glasses of free fizz one can consume (in quick succession on an empty stomach). I would not have questioned this before and would have gone automatically purely for the drinking element.

There are some occasions that I no longer hanker after or choose to sustain. Previously I would arrange regular nights out. Girls' nights out, work nights out for people leaving, passing exams, nights out with my neighbours, with school mums, with old friends and with new friends. My intentions were good. I enjoyed everything about going out, the getting ready, meeting up, the chat, the confidences shared as the alcohol flowed and inhibitions diminished. And of course I enjoyed the opportunity to drink lots. But I hated the day after. It was always the same. The monster hangover always crippling. I despaired of myself, bewildered that I could keep stupidly repeating the same mistake time and again.

Only now can I see that these nights were never really about the people nor the event being marked. They were always about the booze, often only about the booze, and were manufactured to facilitate excessive intake. I have since found it eminently possible to spend time with those I really want to, but in different situations not involving booze. I do 'walk and talk' with some friends, I go to the cinema with others. I enjoy book club and I have been for a catch up chat over a sophisticated afternoon tea. Much more enjoyable and no price to pay the next day. If you had promised me that this would be possible before, I would not have believed you.

Chapter 7 Then and Now: Stress

One of the main reasons cited for drinking alcohol is to relax and relieve stress. I was no different. I am good at compartmentalising my life and my wind down from work involved peace and quiet, and wine. I would arrive home and straight away pour the wine. I would make no move to cook dinner, just continue to drink and snack all evening. I would not deal with the stress or discuss my day. I would simply blot it out, claiming I did not want to go through it all again in conversation. I would keep it blotted out until it passed. Sometimes I would get much coveted peace and quiet. Arrive home to an empty house. Get the glass of wine poured, sit down and after a couple of sips think 'Right, what now? It did not fill the void or meet my need. I could only think that to do so would require more and more. So I had more and more. Did it make me feel better? No. It made me feel worse.

Around ten weeks of alcohol abstinence I had a day at work that I knew would be particularly stressful, challenging me in my weaker areas. It had been fixed in the calendar for a long time, long before I stopped drinking. The day in question fell on a Tuesday and I knew I would have, would need, at least a bottle of wine that evening. In preparation I had booked the following day off work to allow for my hangover. When the day arrived however, I was ten weeks into my new regime and was going to have to manage without the help of alcohol.

Then

I would have had wine to relax the night before and calm my nerves (and blot out my anxious thoughts pertaining to the next day). Anxiety and alcohol would sabotage my sleep leaving me tired, groggy and not at all refreshed. Despite feeling below par, the next day would run competently and be completed but I would feel more stressed by minor problems than need be.

By evening I would feel exhausted from the combination of booze the night before, poor sleep and a difficult day. The solution was to drink more wine. By then I certainly deserved it. At home I wanted to be left alone to escape into the first glass, then the second, then into wine world where nothing else matters and responsibilities slide. I resented my usual chores that were still required, I resented having to interact with my family. Only after three glasses would my tales of the day spew forth. My diatribe once started was continuous. As the wine bottle emptied I would move onto gin and tonic, the quantity consumed being far less obvious than opening a second bottle of wine. Drinking, talking and snacking would continue until bedtime and the next day would be a self fulfilled prophecy, another wipe out day.

Now

I felt anxious the night before. I felt it properly, in harsh reality no longer blotting it out with a bottle of wine. I sat with the uncomfortable feeling, thinking through the day to come, imagining what I would do, how I would deal with the people and the problems, how I wanted to be perceived. My sleep was patchy and I awoke early, keen to get going. I arrived early, motivated and a bit buzzy. I managed the day better than expected albeit notably running on adrenaline at top speed. Afterwards I still felt exhausted but slightly exhilarated too. I had managed and the project had been successful. It would be normal to take the team for a drink after such a day but luckily, the department was out of town, everyone was driving and a trip to the pub was not logistically possible. I said goodbye to a colleague as she got into her car. She wound down the window and said, 'We all deserve a big glass of wine tonight after that, don't we?'

I drove home. At this point I felt something was missing. That I had something to celebrate and could not do so in the traditional way. The day felt unfinished. A fleeting thought of never being able to celebrate with a glass of anything alcoholic ever again panicked me until I dismissed it for now. Once home I did not sit down and I did not want a cup of tea. I felt edgy and could not unwind nor relax into the evening. Again I felt this feeling and acknowledged it. Only now can I see I had been using alcohol to improve my bad times and to relax with the good times. How can one substance do both? I endured my agitation, fidgeting around the house, having a ginger beer and lime and waiting for my brain to stop whirring. It took several hours, until bed time was imminent, when I began to feel safe. My danger hours of early evening had passed and I had reached the time of night that was safe for me. My sensible head would overrule the cravings with the 'What's the point now?' attitude that I believed in. I went to bed satisfied I had managed without. I could still think back on my day clearly and was ready to sleep soundly. This would have been unthinkable less than three months ago

The next day was not one of my 'write off' days of zero achievement and depression. My self satisfaction was amplified and I took to blogging on Soberistas to tell the world how clever I was. As my celebration of this achievement continued in my mind it became tinged with a little bit of sadness. I was sad this was such a big deal for me. Going without alcohol for this one night was a huge deal precisely because it had become such an integral part of my life. When had this happened? Why had I allowed it in so far, to take over? The more I achieved on my sober mission the more I realised that drinking wine had become the biggest most important part of my life. Even the small mundane parts of everyday life were significantly different now that alcohol was removed, leaving behind a huge void.

Chapter 8 Then and Now: Problems and Depression

Alcohol and depression have an intertwined relationship. Alcohol can cause depression and having depression may lead to excessive drinking as a means of self-medicating or a perceived way of coping. The chicken and egg scenario is hard to untangle and will be different between individuals. Trying to treat or improve depression whilst continuing to drinking alcohol is akin to driving with the handbrake on. Let it off, and have the best chance of success without impediment.

When chronically drinking alcohol it is difficult to differentiate true clinical depression from the chronic low grade tiredness and 'cannot be bothered' mentality that is borne of a body under strain to continually metabolise a poison. Many of the symptoms are the same. Alcohol is a depressant drug and depresses our systems. In the very early stages of intake, alcohol depresses our inhibitory messaging channels first allowing the balance to tip in favour of excitatory brain activity and a 'high' feeling. This is transient and very quickly as blood alcohol concentration rises, all neural activity is depressed. This makes us slow, tired, unhappy, nauseous, dehydrated. We become drowsy then comatose, when tragedy can easily occur. Repeating this pattern regularly will see you progress to the next stage of illness when organs begin to fail and suddenly you have serious health issues.

Then

While drinking, my life looked perfect on paper yet in reality, was far from it. I was not happy. I was never content. I felt unable to cope with major stresses, and minor stressors would evoke an angry overreaction. I could not fathom the problem. Why should there be such a discrepancy? I had no money worries, no relationship worries, we were all healthy. I ate well and exercised regularly but remained miserable. I tried lots of things to improve my life. I worked more, then I worked less. I found a cleaning lady for my home and then decided cleaning was therapeutic and did it myself. I lurched from being too busy and stressed to being bored and depressed. I seemed unable to find the mid point where life should be good.

So I drank to improve my life and I drank to escape from it.

My life was so awful this was the least I deserved. Proper grown up 'me' time. The solution for me was to escape from my life as it was, as often as possible, by any means available. Thus I went out a lot, I went away on many work trips and when at home I removed myself by drinking my way into a hazy world of wine where everything was taken down a notch or two. Wine was the only solution. I remember once thinking that the only time I was truly happy was when I was drinking wine in peace and quiet.

Even then I knew this logic was flawed. As I sat with my wine, in peace and quiet I was bored. What now? Drink more wine? But I cannot drink too fast, need to make it last. Playing with my phone was boring and anything else required concentration that I lacked when drinking wine. So, more wine? Would more wine makes things even better, more quickly? Would it magically solve all my problems?

The only problem that wine solves is that caused by lack of wine in the first place. When the body is craving alcohol once again, wine will indeed quell that craving, for a short time and appear to be solving the problem. All other problems are not helped by wine. They are avoided, postponed, and compounded, but never solved by wine. I thought wine helped me to cope with my problems and was what I deserved having to deal with so many. But that was wrong.

Between three and six months of sobriety, as my alcohol induced depressive state resolved, I began to see that wine was actually the cause of my problems and my general dissatisfaction with life, rather than the solution. This realisation made me sad. I was sad I could no longer have wine and I was even sadder that it would not do as I hoped. It would not solve the current problems or help them. All it would do is blot them out for a time, then leave me even less able to cope with them.

Now

I am happier and content. I enjoy my life. It still throws many problems at me, big and small. The small ones I can deal with easily. I sort them out simply and sensibly, and think of the storm in a teacup I would previously have made. Larger problems seem diminished. They are no longer overwhelming. My first thought is always 'Thank goodness I don't have a hangover to deal with too'. Procrastination has gone and I can get on with things directly, thinking clearly and rationally. I am no longer engulfed in an all-consuming calamity. When problems arise I can detach and wonder if it will actually matter in five years time. I can accept a less than perfect solution, knowing it is good enough. I have time to think and have capacity in my brain to do so, since it is no longer preoccupied with the continual planning, buying, drinking or suffering from, wine. I can concentrate now. I have more patience. I am interested in my family and spending time interacting with them. I feel stable and level, not on an up nor a down. I just am. I just can. And I do. I can do lots more now my day is not truncated at six o'clock to drink wine. Why did I ever drink? Why did I not see alcohol as the villain? Paradoxically thinking it was exactly the tonic required rather than the last thing I needed.

Chapter 9 Then and Now: Travelling for Work

As I approached the three month mark of breaking free from the clutches of alcohol I had a major challenge to my on-going sobriety. I had to attend a conference with work. It would last two days and two nights and involve travel, staying away from home in a hotel. And alcohol. Lots of it. I used to think I enjoyed being away with work but this time I was nervous. In the very early days of abstinence I had marked this trip as a potential event where I could return to wine if I chose to do so. It was close to my planned three month reassessment. Now this point in time had arrived I decided I wanted to remain sober for just a bit longer. I wanted to survive this event without alcohol this year. At the back of my mind I was reassured. This was an annual event. I had spent plenty of them drunk and convivial so I planned to spend this one sober. If it was awful missing out the drinking aspect of it, I could always revert to my usual ways next year. Meetings, conferences and hotel stays equate to drinks in the bar when the work is finished, a drink in the room while getting ready for the evening, pre-dinner drinks, wine with dinner, night caps back at the hotel bar. Late nights and hangovers were the norm.

Then

We travelled as a group of colleagues to the city hosting the conference. The train was known colloquially as the red wine express and we were like children going on a school trip. We would check into the hotel then attend the conference, only to leave again before the final session of the day in order to bond in a nearby pub. After a couple of hours we would go back to the hotel for a quick shower and change before meeting in the bar before dinner. I would be buzzing by this point. Still on a high from the afternoon drinks, the low not yet begun. An empty stomach ensured the alcohol fast-tracked to my brain and I was full of anticipation for the big night out, what may happen, how it would evolve, what fun we would have. I would get ready quickly, my flushed face requiring little make up, being less bothered about my hair looking just right. I never stopped to think how the evening would end, I just wanted to get down to the bar and continue on my merry way.

Dinner was a big affair with pre dinner drinks and copious wine throughout. At the end of the evening we would stagger back to the hotel, complete now with our exaggerated camaraderie and great statements of mutual friendship, respect and admiration.

The next day was a struggle. We would often miss the first session of the conference to have a full english breakfast. This started a day of over eating for me in a vain attempt to quell the waves of nausea with sugar, fat and carbohydrates. Gossip ensued, recounting tales of the night before, who was in the worst state, who had not made it to breakfast. Lethargy was compounded by a day of lectures necessitating an early return to the hotel for a quick nap before the second night out. I would always plan to take it easy on the first night so as to be able to enjoy the second night too but this never went according to plan. The second night was always a let down despite consisting of a quality dinner in a formal venue necessitating a dress and heels. I was subdued as yet further alcohol intake accumulated and the unpleasant feeling prevailed of drinking again while still hungover. It was unthinkable not to drink at these events. Everyone drank, many excessively. What would you do if not drinking? Being away from home and freed from those commitments, it seemed that no other rules or restraints applied either. My time was my own and I used it to drink. All my irresponsible tendencies could roam free. No one was driving. No one had meetings or early starts the next day. I would lose count of what I had to drink, until it was too late.

I would sleep poorly. Tossing and turning, feeling unwell, restless, awful. Lurching from worry that I had gone too far in front of work colleagues to despair that once again I never knew when enough was enough.

The following morning I would gingerly assess my level of function. If I could get to the breakfast room I would sit hidden in a corner with my back to the room, unable to face chit chat. We would catch the return train home, a more subdued bunch than the day we arrived. I would quietly contemplate my headache, lament that yet again it was not worth it, and berate myself about how awful I felt. Never forgetting to vow never to drink that much again.

I would arrive home to a rapturous reception while feeling like death inside. I would try to pass it off as 'tired from all that travelling'. All I wanted to do was be left alone and to go to bed at an unreasonably early hour but my family had missed me and insisted I partake in a round of bathtime and bedtime hilarity.

Now

If I was to succeed this year I had to plan in advance. Leaving anything to chance was too risky as I did not trust myself to be strong at moments of temptation. I planned a mixture of avoidance, distraction and alternative options to take the place of drinking.

I claimed domestic responsibilities and left home on a later train, thus travelling alone. It provided a few hours of solitude to read and think and remind myself of why I was choosing to do things differently this time. I avoided the 'free' drinks on the train and the incessant chat of the partying plan. I arrived without a promise to get to the bar as soon as possible. I stayed all afternoon at the conference and walked back to the hotel with a friend. Stating phone calls to be made, I excused myself from the first bar trip. I took my time getting ready, made an effort to look nice and reminded myself I would look exactly the same at the end of the evening. No wardrobe or bodily malfunctions would occur. I enjoyed the certainty of knowing I would be back at a reasonable hour and in control.

I chose to avoid the main protagonists of excess and stuck more closely to a few quieter ones in the group. For us it was a civilised, low key night and whatever we each were drinking or not, was never a big issue. Drinking was not the focus here. It was all about eating an evening meal, away from home, with colleagues. Quite straight forward really.

I enjoyed the second day at the conference and looked forward to the formal night with a mixture of excitement at the challenge and apprehension about going and remaining stone cold sober. I logged on to the Soberistas website in my hotel room and asked for support and advice. I had the support of many well-wishers who asked me to check back in later when the night was over.

It would be very embarrassing to return with failure to report. Even with the relative anonymity of the web, I felt accountable to those supporting me and did not want to let them down.

One supporter suggested escaping from the event for a period of time if it was awful or even just to pass some time. Go outside, make a phone call or take a book and stay reading in the lobby or the Ladies for half an hour, surf the web or come and chat on the website. Others, once drunk would not notice my prolonged absence and it would remove me for a while from the environment where the drink was flowing.

I went to the formal dinner in the last taxi to leave the hotel thus avoiding the pre-pre-dinner drinks and limiting the time available to spend at the drinks reception. On arrival I took a glass of orange juice in a champagne flute and began to mingle. I felt truly awkward, kind of wooden and all out of place. Everything about me seemed so conspicuous; the way I was standing, the way I was looking around, the way I was talking. I did not enjoy it and was pleased when we were asked to sit down.

I fail to understand the point of pre dinner drinks if not to loosen the guests up with alcohol on an empty stomach. I guess it is part of hospitality, offering a drink while waiting for all the guests to arrive but I still did not enjoy this brief part of the evening at all.

We sat at the tables and again I avoided my usual crowd of like-minded individuals and sat next to people I knew less well. One chap seemed to know me really well and was very friendly and complimentary. I was flattered and surprised until I saw how much he was drinking and realised that he was, actually, very drunk. The food seemed to take forever to arrive and the table was crowded with wine. The only other option was water which I was not exactly thrilled about. I left the table to go to the bar and buy a diet coke. I was distinctly unimpressed that while the wine was free, I had to pay for a soft drink. But it was nice and I enjoyed it and it passed some time before the meal arrived. I ate my meal and laughed off the assumption I must be pregnant when my coke was noted. My family are well past the baby stage and I am the wrong side of forty for another pregnancy.

Conversation at the table took a lot of effort. The venue was noisy and it was difficult to be heard. Never a problem I would notice when wine was flowing in the past, presumably everyone just gets louder and louder as the night wears on. Or perhaps when drinking alcohol you are less inclined to actually listen and to want to hear what another is saying so the volume does not matter so much. But I actively tried to maintain a conversation with my dinner companions throughout the meal, above the din.

After dinner I listened to the speech. It went on a while. It was difficult to tell if it was too long or that I was more aware of its duration not using the time to quietly drink more wine. When it ended I got up from the table and went outside, along with all the smokers. It was ten o'clock so I phoned home, I checked my emails and texted a few friends. By the time I went back inside people were awaiting transport back to the hotel. For me it could not arrive quickly enough but I watched others rush to finish their drinks before leaving, horrified to be leaving while bottles of wine lay unfinished. I admit I felt slightly superior. We got back to the hotel and half of my group went to the hotel bar and the other half, me included, pleaded tiredness and went to bed. I got into my room and breathed a sigh of relief.

I had survived intact. It had been an endurance though, and as I had my tea and chocolates in bed I thought how different the night had been without alcohol. On the surface I thought it was much less fun but wondered, how much fun was there to be had anyway? Undoubtedly the first couple of drinks are enjoyable (although in fact only because they feed the alcohol craving), that floaty bubbly feeling of being on your way. Even when it progresses to that dreamy stage where everything seems warm and cosy. But that was all. What I called fun was getting more and more drunk in the company of others doing the same. Without the drinking element I found I had little in common with many and did not want to prolong my time in their company. I had been bored at times during the evening. Was the event itself a bit boring or was it me who was boring without a drink? If so, I did not really care, but it was not me. It is just that when the focus is alcohol, it masks the boring reality of life. Being occupied by drinking and getting drunk meant I never stopped to think about how boring or otherwise the occasion was; it was merely a platform on which to drink. It probably would not have mattered where we were, as long as there was a plentiful supply of booze. So I agreed with myself it was not the 'fun' that I was missing. I felt very sensible too. I was back at a reasonable hour, without misdemeanor. Did I miss the wildness of my old ways? I admit I did in part although not enough to want them back along with the accompanying negative aspects which outlast any small amount of pleasure. I definitely felt this new way was much more befitting of my age and stage in life and my personal and professional status.

I checked in on-line with the well wishing Soberistas. It was nice to have 'someone' with whom to share my victory. I fell asleep incredibly happy, pleased, relieved that I would not be hungover the next day.

My travel home was enjoyable. On a train surrounded by people suffering from their over indulgence the night before I felt even happier. Their 'fun' was over whereas mine continued. I now keep these trips to a minimum, only going away from home when I absolutely have to. I realise they served as a licence for me to drink continually and excessively. Being away from family commitments, chores and children, my time was my own to drink, be hungover and subsequently overeat. This time I felt relaxed and was happily looking forward to arriving home. I was not exhausted nor worn out and I felt truly deserving of the unconditional welcome I received when I walked through the front door.

Chapter 10 Then and Now: Holidays.

Alcohol has always been a significant part of any holiday I have had. Ditching the alcohol at the start of my all inclusive trip earlier in the year was a huge change. In part it was possible for me as it was an altogether new holiday experience, not one I had done each year and grown to associate with an established drinking pattern.

Each year we have a two week break in the sun mid-July. We choose self catering accommodation and it is a pool and beach type holiday. We usually stay and play or read around the pool by day and eat out for dinner most evenings.

Then

Soon after arrival we would do a big shop for essential items. Among these I would include alcohol. I would check out the local wine selection and buy some cans of slimline tonic to have with my bottle of gin purchased at the duty free. I would start to drink most days in the afternoon, at ice cream time. Rather than having an ice cream I would claim to prefer a refreshing beer. I would ask OH casually if he fancied one too and usually, he did not. I was then embarrassed to be drinking a beer as the others had ice creams and I was also embarrassed when the bartender assumed it would be a half pint for me, presumably because its not usual to see the mother having a pint. I felt greedy and needy asking for a whole pint. All these awkward moments would not, however, be enough to deter me if my mind was made up.

Then it was a case of coasting along until we had enough sun and went back indoors, to get showered and changed. Sometimes this would be my first drink of the day and I would have a home poured gin and tonic. I would post-pone going for a shower while I had the first drink and would top it up with a lot of gin and a little tonic while the others were busy changing. I would be feeling slightly drunk and pleasantly happy on our way out to a restaurant. I would then proceed to drink only a normal amount with the meal, perhaps sharing a bottle of wine. This would mean my OH having a glass and perhaps a small top up, and me having the rest of the bottle.

When we returned to our apartment I would want to sit quietly out on the balcony with another drink. I did not stop to think of how I would feel the next day, or if I did, I was blasé and dismissed those thoughts for now; I could worry about them tomorrow. I would be torn between wanting to read my novel but knowing that tomorrow I would not remember the bits I read and I did not want to miss out on the plot. At times of such drunkenness I could become argumentative, often 'stressed' and have toddler-like tantrums. I look back to how irresponsible and irrational my behaviour was and wonder that my OH put up with it.

The day after I would be grumpy, munchy, irritable and tired, until the afternoon rolled around when it would be time to start all over again. Throughout the two weeks my OH would have a few nights off, not drinking at all. I never did, I was on holiday after all. I still got bored drinking night after night in the same way, doing the same thing but it would never occur to me that going without was an option for me too. It was so easy, having a fridge and a supply of booze, too easy and I still thought that the more I drank the better the time would be had.

Now

This year when our summer holiday came around I had been off alcohol for almost four months. Again, it was a point in time I had earmarked as 'giving up until'. By now I was reluctant to throw away all that I had achieved to date. To put all my efforts aside and revert to the same old, same old. I was remembering our earlier holiday during my first two weeks of sobriety and that I had enjoyed it and had fun. I had not needed alcohol for that element. I now perceived alcohol as much less of a treat I was denying myself and creating more of a risk to my well being. I really wanted to try this holiday alcohol free. It would be another first and if it was awful, I could always go back to drinking next year. But still, it would be my biggest challenge yet.

I have often bemoaned the fact that my OH does not drink vey much or very often. I have thought him boring and no fun at all at party time. This way of his though, was a huge help to me in avoiding the drink. He was often not bothered and would not drink anyway, making it easier for me to do the same. Again the first night out for dinner was brief as we were tired. I did not want to drink that night but knew I might the next night and I would consider it again when the time came. The next two nights I did not drink alcohol but I found I did not enjoy the overall experience of going out for dinner nearly as much. The focus had obviously been with wine before now and I did not enjoy my sparkling water as a pre-dinner drink. This, as well as the fact that we had a well-equipped villa meant we had our evening meal at home more often. Without a hangover I was unusually content to potter about in the kitchen preparing our dinner to eat out on the terrace. I did not feel the same harassed need-to-get-away and switch off from it all, (whatever 'it' is) with alcohol in a restaurant. My days were glorious. I would awaken early, feeling bright and optimistic about the day. I often walked along the beach before breakfast and before it got too hot. By the pool I found myself willing to play catch, ping pong and spend time with my children rather than being slumped on a lounger willing my headache to go. There also seemed to be less of a rush, the timetable was less important when I was not drinking. I'm not sure why but I felt I could go with the flow. What we did and when we did it no longer seemed to matter. I had no ulterior agenda to accommodate. This year I had the best holiday of my life. I came home glowing, without a weight gain, feeling invincible.

Later in the year, when I had been sober for six months, we had a weekend away at a holiday village. We do this once or twice throughout the year during school holidays and our routine is always fairly consistent. We rent a log cabin and do a mixture of self-catering and eating out.

Then

My last trip there before I removed alcohol from my life was fairly typical. I had been flirting with alcohol avoidance in the lead up period and had abstained for a couple of weeks. My 'reward' for this effort was to drink as I normally did during this three night break. So we arrived on Friday at lunchtime and headed straight to the swimming pool. We spent the afternoon there indulging the kids all the while managing the anticipation of that first glass. We stop off at the supermarket then head on over to our chalet. We unload the car and I start unpacking the food box first. It contains several bottles of wine, the result of much consideration before we left home. Three days, three bottles? No, OH may

92

want some too so better take a spare as well. But going out for dinner at least one night which will lend itself to additional wine purchasing and drinking so maybe take one less? Then again will no doubt want more to drink when we arrive home from the restaurant so will still need that extra one. These long drawn out thought processes were the norm.

As I unpacked and started to make dinner for the children I would have my first glass of wine. It would be surreptitiously topped up in the kitchen to blur the number of glasses being consumed (to me and anyone else interested). This would continue while the kids ate and OH sorted out the car. Our dinner was delayed as I messed around in the kitchen drinking wine, prolonging the cooking. We sat down with a drink and dinner. A couple of drinks with dinner was acceptable but if OH chose wine instead of beer it became more obvious that the bottle emptied very quickly. After dinner he would move onto coffee and chocolate while herding the children through their bathroom and bedtime routine. I would be onto the next bottle, becoming increasingly annoyed with the presence of the kids and their excitement at being on holiday. We would plan to watch a movie both knowing I would fall asleep on the sofa near the beginning of it. When it finished I would wake up and move to the bedroom, stopping for a large glass of water on the way, feeling regret that I had missed the film.

The next day I would assess my hangover and be pleased to be functional. I would have extra toast at breakfast before we returned to the swimming pool. The children love it so I would put up with being there. I was always grumpy, in need of carbs and wondering when in the day I would feel well enough to start drinking again. The pool was followed by ten pin bowling. The best thing about bowling is its association with a pint of lager. Thus lager was drunk mid afternoon as a little extra, being additional to the evening's quota of wine. So at four o'clock I put up with the noisy dark environment, do the bowling and try to drink more slowly than my OH and make my pint last for the full hour (OH would drink slowly and I would be too embarrassed to get another drink alone). After that pint, the want was well and truly unleashed. I hated the hiatus between drinks so when the bowling was over and we moved upstairs to an Italian restaurant for dinner. I was desperate to be served quickly. I wanted our drink order to be taken immediately while the menus were being handed around. OH would stick with beer and I would move onto wine. I didn't want to peruse the wine list in case the waitress left and offered to come back, to give me a chance to study it. No, I just wanted it fast. Despite the comparable amount in a bottle of wine, I would order only a glass (and pretend to consider the question 'large or small' before smiling and choosing the large one, just this once, justifying it with a 'Go on then, I am on holiday after all'). A large glass was one third of a bottle and I would usually have two glasses, or sometimes three. It seemed less obvious than overtly drinking a whole bottle of wine on my own in a restaurant. I would always be aware of how far through a glass I was, how to catch the waitress' eye, and how I must look to OH and to others.   Again after dinner the walk home brought another hiatus. I felt rushed to get home and get settled with another glass. There may be a glass left from the second bottle of the previous night. It would be disappointing. It would not taste good as it had been open for 24 hours and it would not taste good as I had already had too much. Diminishing returns. My mood would deteriorate as my want could not be met and the void, whatever its cause, was not being successfully filled by drinking more wine. I would repeat my fall asleep on the sofa and go to bed with a large glass of water.

The next day, the third and final of the break, would see me suffering an increasingly bad hangover compounded by two days' drinking. I would want things to remain low key, not wanting to be bothered with or to interact with family life. Rather I just wanted to get through the day. I was worried about dinner time. We were going out for a Sunday roast in the pub at five o'clock. I would drink again then and while my stomach did not feel quite up to it, my brain could not conceive the event without alcohol. This turmoil was on my mind all day. Did I need to drink that night? No, but I seemed incapable of actioning that rational thought. I could not bear to allow a drinking opportunity like this to pass without drinking, and when the time came for the first 'What are you having to drink?' I resigned myself to another large glass of wine, almost against my better judgement. This time, not even the first glass was enjoyable. I sipped it tentatively wondering whether it would make me feel better or worse. Soon I would head to the carvery for my roast dinner. After eating, I would be overfull and my second glass of wine would make me even more uncomfortable. I had made lots of poor choices and was feeling rotten, both physically and mentally. Why stop now? I may as well continue and have dessert too. Once back at our accommodation I knew I should call it a night but a part bottle of wine remained in the fridge and we were going home the next morning. Thinking it would be a shame to waste it, I would drink it too.

The next morning we got ready to travel home. I felt low, exhausted, fraught with the organisation of it all. I fell asleep during the car journey home and continued my self abuse with an excess of carbs and chocolate once home.

I would usually manage to stay alcohol free that night, in preparation for going back to work the next day and also in an attempt to let time pass and the hangover recede.

Now

Around six months free from alcohol we did exactly the same break. It was the first trip where I was confident in myself and my plan to remain alcohol free. I had a mild degree of anxiety. It was after all, another set of 'firsts' to be tackled alcohol free but by now I was getting so much better at managing these.

The first afternoon trip to the supermarket surprised me. It was 5pm. It was growing dark outside. I was waiting in the queue alone with my thoughts when the idea of wine appeared. It just seemed everything was colluding to take my thoughts to wine and how it would usually feature in this set of circumstances. I could see it in others' baskets, I could see it on the shelves and I knew I did not have any in my basket, in the food box or in the accommodation. However, it was just that, a thought. Only a thought. A thought that could be managed and limited. Thoughts can lead to feelings and feelings lead to actions. This thought led to feelings of desire, of something being missing, something I had once been close to, and of a wish that things had turned out differently. Crucially these thoughts and feelings did not lead to action. I did not buy or seek wine and the moment passed and life went on.

It is novel to sit with feelings that are uncomfortable when we are used to the instant solution of using alcohol to push them down. Many reformed drinkers talk about the need to 'feel, deal, heal'. Having to allow their emotions room to occur and display, having to address them head on and deal with their meaning all without resorting to their usual vice is a significant part of their recovery. Difficult feelings can be acknowledged, sat with, allowed to exist by remembering always, that these too will pass. And in the supermarket they did pass. Back at the chalet I busied myself unpacking and making dinner pleased that the moment had jumped out, catching me unawares, and I had survived unscathed.

The next day we had our regular ten pin bowling. I was struck with thoughts of my usual lager and lime. It was just part of that whole situation. Part of the habit. But this time there was no debate, no 'will I won't I' to oscillate between. I simply ordered a soda and lime and was surprised that it tasted nice and I really enjoyed it. It was refreshing and it was of no consequence that I drank half of the pint in a matter of minutes.

Onwards to the Italian restaurant for dinner. I was more relaxed without the wine, more going with the flow. There was so much less to think about inside my head, I was no longer pre-occupied with wine. I felt more present in the moment, the conversation and the interaction of being part of a family. I was more interested in the menu now that I was no longer trying to postpone the arrival of food, to have more time for wine beforehand. I wasn't bothered by the slow service which eventually brought our drinks. I wasn't worried what others were thinking about my drinking, my OH, the waiters. I have never enjoyed the combination of wine and dessert, it was always one or the other and the wine always won. This time I enjoyed dessert. I did not need to prolong the dinner and delay our departure, the kids bored and restless, while I finished off my wine. I was happy to leave once we had eaten. We cycled home detouring to take a longer route. I enjoyed the follow-the-leader-ride. It was exciting, in the dark with our bike lights showing the way ahead. There was no rush to get home. No rush to get the next drink. No rush to get the children packed off to bed and out of the way.

A good sleep and great sense of accomplishment in my sensible choices meant the next day I felt happy and calm and could look forward to enjoying the day's activities rather than enduring them with a clenched, tense jaw and waves of nausea.

I treated myself to an afternoon in the spa. I had only been once before with a like-minded friend and wine remained the focus of the event. We did a quick tour of the saunas and steam rooms before heading to the 'Vitality' cafe which was so healthy it did not sell any form of crisps but had a selection of sophisticated wines. One (large) glass became two (only polite to buy a round each) which led to a disregard for family dinner and evening plans as the time passed. Ultimately, I left disappointed as the 'me' time ended and I had to go back to reality, slightly drunk, wanting more and not interested in the needs of anyone else.

This time going to the spa seemed to be an optional choice for a pleasant solitary break rather than an absolute requirement to escape from family life and snooze off the hangover for a couple of hours.

I felt calm and enjoyed each moment wandering between different saunas, pools and loungers. I was not frantically counting down to the wine time. Afterwards I felt relaxed and invigorated, instead of partially recovered and able to start another round of drinking.

I previously believed the main attraction of places such as Center Parcs was the presence of soft play and child friendly areas in close proximity to cafes and bars which sold alcohol. It capitalised on the myth that parents require alcohol to cope with rearing their children, the myth that relaxing with alcohol was the be all and end all. Objectively, despite the wine, these places still brought disappointment. They are noisy and busy and our real craving when the children are young is not for wine, it is for peace, tranquility and an unbroken night's sleep. The last thing we need is to compound the challenge of children with the debilitation brought on by wine. How are we so blind to that?

Chapter 11 Then and Now : Cinema

My socialising has changed dramatically since dropping the alcohol as you might expect, but has done so in ways which I did not envisage. There are some things I no longer want to do and some I continue with which are entirely different. In this latter category I would include going to the cinema. I previously enjoyed this activity until wine took hold of me and turned this evening into one which did not allow for much drinking, and trying to combine the two seemed endlessly complicated.

Then

The date is a Saturday night. I hope OH will be playing golf early the next day because he doesn't drink the night before playing. He can drive and I can drink. If he wants to drink too we take a car to cinema, then drive to restaurant, leave the car at restaurant and take a taxi home. This necessitates a trip to collect the car the following day. Then there is the order of the evening to consider. Cinema first then dinner to follow means either no drink until about 8.30pm (too late) or an early drink beforehand around 5pm with the evidence cleared away before the babysitter arrives. Then follows an unwelcome enforced break from alcohol while the film is on. Watch the film but disappointed cannot continue to drink. Then we get to restaurant and I order a large glass of wine. I drink quickly and worry about finishing the glass at a time the waiter is not around to bring another swiftly. There is not much babysitting time left so it's a bit of a rush drinking 2 large glasses along with dinner. This spoils the anticipated enjoyment and I do not feel relaxed at all. We arrive home and I want to keep drinking so have another glass while OH is having coffee and a biscuit before bed. I am feeling guilty about having more to drink because, well why would you at that point in the evening?

The reverse option of dinner followed by cinema is no better. The rush to drink lots of wine before movie starts. The annoyance that the movie has interrupted drinking. The sleepiness and lack of concentration during the film. It feels awkward re-starting drinking after a two hour hiatus towards the end of the evening when normal people are having coffee and biscuits before bed but I would manage. The next day is a bit hungover, low of mood, munch-y of food and irritable. I cannot be bothered to do anything.

Now

I drive to cinema, enjoy the film. Drive to the restaurant, relax and enjoy the food. Drive home. Have tea and biscuits before going to bed for a good sleep. I feel great the next morning, I can remember the film while buzzing around the house in full productive mode. Simple.

Chapter 12 Then and Now: Girls' Nights Out

There are some social occasions I remain less confident about. These I avoided until I felt stronger and better able to handle them without defaulting to the common wine pathway. These challenges include nights out (and in) with The Girls and an overnight away with one of my best friends.

I am a part of a group of six friends known as the Chatty Girls. We met long ago at a mother and baby group and have remained friends long since our babies grew up. We meet approximately every two to three months for dinner. We take turns at hosting the evening in each of our homes.

I was long overdue a turn at being host and had been continually putting it off. Truth was I did not feel confident I could manage not to drink in my own home setting. There would be too few barriers to drinking. The wine would be of my choosing and I could roll into bed at the end of the night without any transport issues. These evenings are very sociable. They begin with pink fizz (any type), progress to wine with dinner, continuing afterwards with port, sherry, sloe gin or whatever peculiarity the hostess finds at the back of her drinks cabinet. I have been to one of these nights and not drank alcohol.

Although this was not through choice, I was surprised by how much I enjoyed that evening. Despite this, I would never choose to do it this way. I had mentioned to a couple of the girls that I had stopped drinking but had done so earlier in the year and they assumed it was a short term health kick and it had not been mentioned recently.

By month eight of my alcohol-free life I felt I could put it off no longer and decided to host an evening with the chatty girls in my home.

Then

I would have booked the following day off work in advance of the anticipated hangover or have it scheduled for a Friday night. I would spend the day pottering around, preparing food, tidying up. I would spend a long time deliberating over drinks, glasses, where to serve, what to offer, who would like what. I would set the table, lay out snacks then have a quick shower. I would have my first drink as I got dressed to get me in the mood and then once everything was ready, I would sit down and relax with a large glass of wine, alone and content, before anyone arrived. At the others' homes I would be one of the first to arrive and would take along two nice bottles of wine to ensure there was something I would enjoy: as I started to drink more and more, I began to buy increasingly expensive bottles of wine, trying to find one I would definitely like. I now wonder if this was

106

an early sign of me realising it doesn't actually taste very nice whatever the price. I failed to make that connection at the time.

I would help the host to do drinks as people arrived, continually topping my own up. In my home I would have an additional glass on the go in the kitchen. I would often pretend to be mixed up about which glass was mine, or where I had put it down. I would be fairly quiet for the first part of the evening, content to sit and listen while drinking away my day and relaxing into the blurry cocoon of booze, friends, and friendship. Once sufficiently lubricated I would perk up and become Mrs Chatty. I am always animated but at these times I am sure I become over-bearing, monopolise the conversation, have a rant or exude self-righteousness about something or other. I would enjoy dessert, continuing in my loud something-to-say about everything manner and become a self appointed expert on things I often didn't know much about. Sometimes I would become teary and over emotional, repeating my tales of woe verbatim from the last such evening I had cried and over-shared. By the time the end of meal chocolates came out I would scoff them continually, self control long gone. I would leave with the others, around 1am and crawl into bed knowing the price I would be paying for such over indulgences in a few short hours. In my home I would clear up when they had left, drinking all the while and once finished I would again sit and relax alone, in peace and quiet with another glass of wine and reflect on what a good night we'd had. The next morning I would wonder if I had been too, too much, and be thankful they were clearly very good friends who actually liked me for me, even when drunk.

Now

I have seen these girls twice since stopping drinking. Each time I've driven, arrived last and left first on the pretext of a busy next day or being very tired. Both times I felt as if I missed out on the full experience by not drinking, yet afterwards was pleased I had not. It seemed conflicting. Hosting in my own home would be a whole new minefield. I would have no driving to keep me sober if my will power was failing and I knew there would be a discussion of some sort about me not drinking. They were good friends and I planned to be honest when the topic came up.

In preparation, for the first time in eight months I bought wine with my shopping. I unpacked the bags noticing that the two bottles of white felt chilled already from being outdoors. Condensation had developed on the bottle and droplets ran down the side. It felt heavy in my hand. I looked at it and felt a longing. It brought back a desire I had been ignoring. At that moment I realised how much I had missed wine; much like an old friend I had not seen in a while. Our reunion was tinged by changes to our relationship; here she was yet I had changed, and hard though it may be, our relationship was going to be different. I put the bottles in the cupboard rather than the fridge to reduce the temptation and to keep them out of sight until the day arrived when they would be required.

As the evening approached, I became aware of the huge impact wine once had at this early stage: now, instead of being off duty and out of bounds with regards to the needs of the others in my home, I was able to prepare for guests whilst attending to my family and being with them. I bought wine and had other drinks in the house and cared much less about what everyone might want or think. Everything was so much less of a big deal. My snacks were much simpler. The cooking seemed less stressful. In fact, everything seemed so much easier. I enjoyed the food and sampled it all. This was a joy, as usually my self-imposed calorie restriction meant wine or food and previously my choice had always been for wine. I did not feel the awkward awareness brought about by the absence of alcohol that I had felt previously at pre-dinner drinks receptions or in a restaurant. Partly I was busy hosting and partly my priority was genuinely to hear the girls' news and I was happy doing that. It did not need any drug to make it better. I was not annoyed by the interruptions my family made throughout the evening. I continued to be an understanding compassionate mother who could make time for them, rather than my wine fixated alter ego wishing to be left alone by my normal mundane life.

I was a good host, polite and attentive and for once did not sneak into the kitchen for secret chats and extra drinks with any one of my friends. I did not encourage others to drink more than they were doing themselves.

I was asked if I was still not drinking by one friend whom I had told some time before. General shock was apparent on the faces of those who did not know I had ever stopped. Apparently, for me to stop drinking was unthinkable.

"How long for?"

"Why?"

"I thought you had G and T earlier?" (No, just sparkling water.)

"Do you feel better?"

"When will you re-start? It's Christmas soon."

All the questions rushed forth at once. I replied that I thought I was drinking too much. I had been chronically tired, irritable and feeling down. I thought a period without alcohol may help. I had read you need a period of at least three months abstinence to notice a difference, but six months was better. At three months it had seemed possible to commit to another three and here I was at eight months. I said aloud that I would not go back to it now, I did not really miss it and saw no reason to re-introduce it to my life. I did not divulge how difficult I still found this. How much I planned, worried, thought about it, was tempted by it and how I was not always completely convinced that life actually was better without it, some of the time at least. I was still hoping that if I said it often enough I would eventually believe it but for now, I did not feel secure enough to tell the whole stark truth.

There was a few 'Good for yous' and overall they appeared impressed, seeing this as a positive change I had chosen to make, rather than truly knowing that I was drinking far too much, was worried I had a problem, could not control it and felt I had no option but to enforce total abstinence.

By ten o'clock the meal was over and we were back in the lounge. I wanted a big cup of tea but felt it too early to offer tea and coffee, as if to round off the evening. I made it for myself and said I was not rushing anyone and would do coffee later. One friend said, 'Great, we have booked a taxi for midnight'.

Midnight seemed a long time away and indeed it was a long time away. As the time passed I had too many cups of tea and became more and more tired. The others however became more and more animated, their laughter getting louder and louder as they finished off various bottles of booze.

I was not the party pooper but I did realise the night was well and truly over some time earlier and I just wanted them to leave.

We had shared our news, had a meal, spent time discussing our lives and up-coming plans. There was nothing more to add. It was purely extra drinking time. I tidied up as the time edged closer to midnight and went to bed swiftly after they left.

The next day I did not need to lie quietly on the sofa hoping the children would leave me alone and I did not need an afternoon snooze. I washed the glasses hating the smell of stale alcohol left in them and met all my family commitments as planned that day. I felt I had the best of both worlds.

There is a bottle of white wine left. I have kept it for the next time people visit. The allure has diminished somewhat further. I did not need it and had a great night without it.

I hope my friends still enjoy my company now I am sober. I am afraid to ask outright but I feel that sober, my best bits remain and the uglier side of me is kept well away. Surely this can only be a good thing?

I have another Girls' Night Out with my running (or more usually, walking) friend. We meet once a week for an hour of walk and talk and have come to know each other well, failings and all. We go out together infrequently but the object is always to drink a lot of wine, go a bit wild, compare hangovers the next day and try to remember why it was such a great night. I told her I had stopped drinking for much the same reasons I had told the Chatty Girls, the difference being this time, both she and I know we each drink too much. I first told her I had given up drinking after about six weeks. I was feeling quite proud of myself and she was one of the first people I told. She burst out laughing and said, 'Yeah sure you have'. The wind was ripped from my sails and I was swiftly deflated. She noticed my crest-fallen look and immediately apologised for being so presumptuous and unsupportive. Periodically she asks if I am still 'off the wine' as if knowing it cannot last indefinitely.

We have not had a night out together since I stopped drinking and I do not feel the need to do so. Our friendship exists perfectly well walking around the park having an hour of mutually therapeutic chat and fresh air. She often jokes about things we will do 'once you're back on the wine' and if we go skiing together next year 'you'll need to be back on the wine by then'. I know I will not be back on the wine and hopefully that will matter less and less as time goes on. I fear she may have lost a drinking partner but kept a good friend.

My all-time best friend lives far from me and we do not see each other very often. We are very similar in our outlook, our thoughts, our profession. Our meetings are few and far between and have to be planned well in advance. They count as 'special occasions' and are maximised by having an overnight hotel stay (sharing a twin room), excessive chatting and of course copious drinking.

A meet up of this kind had been planned earlier in the year and I was seven months sober when it arrived. We checked into the hotel and had a chat. We planned our evening around dinner, chatting, magazines and television. It was a fairly formal place so we opted for more casual bar food at five o'clock rather than dinner in the restaurant. We ordered the afternoon tea and relaxed into massive comfortable armchairs by a roaring fire. As we chatted I brought up the subject of my continued abstinence. This was my closest friend and I could tell her anything without judgement.

'I've stopped drinking,' I said.

'Have you? Why is that?'

I stated my usual line about tiredness and mood but added, for the first time, that I was drinking too much, had failed at moderation and felt total abstinence was now my only option. She is perhaps, in a similar boat, I'm not sure, but we had a good conversation about how hard life feels and how there is often a perceived need to collapse with a deserving glass of wine at the end of each and every day. Our pot of tea grew cold and I asked if she wanted a drink from the bar, as I was going to get a diet coke. She admitted to really wanting a glass of wine but felt she couldn't as I wasn't drinking with her. I said not to be silly; I didn't mind if she drank, and hoped she didn't mind that I didn't.

So she had a glass a wine, I had a diet coke and then we called it a night, both happy.

I felt I had taken my first step towards coming out honestly.

Chapter 13 Coming Out

By eight months it was becoming easier to automatically know I no longer drank alcohol. Alcoholic occasions seemed less of a challenge and the decision whether to drink or not receded. There was no decision to be made; I didn't drink. I continued to notice small differences this made. As I was booking a Friday night off work for a night out I had automatically requested no shifts on the Saturday or Sunday either. I smiled as I realised this was no longer necessary. I would not have a monster hangover. Instead I would be fit and able to work the day after if required to do so.

I had been gradually telling more and more people that I did not drink. I started to drop it into conversations with people whom I knew did not drink either, and to people who did not know me very well and would accept what I said at face value. One new member of a committee I am on lives near me. I had given her a lift home one night and as she thanked me she said she would drive us both the next time. I told her I didn't drink and would be happy to drive us both again.

A few days later at our coffee break we were discussing the possibility of having wine at the Christmas lunch. There was still work to be done in the afternoon and this new person said she would have to drive home anyway, until I reminded her that I could give her a lift.

'I forgot you don't drink,' she said

The others, including a good friend, immediately turned to me in a mixture of confusion, surprise and amazement.

'Since when?' someone challenged me,

'What, not at all?'

'Why?' they asked.

I answered that it was making me feel chronically irritable and depressed so I was having some time away from it. Making such a definitive statement to people I know well felt very high stakes. There really would be no going back now. I could not imagine giving them explanations of why I may later be drinking again, if I was found myself doing so. If telling these people had happened earlier along the way I would have felt pressurised and at risk of failure, unsure if I could cope or actually do it in the long term. But now I felt it was an affirmation aloud of what I had been doing and the way I now lived. I didn't cut the conversation short but I was glad when the topic changed and I was no longer in the spotlight. I have since met a friend from this group alone and it was notable that she did not mention this change. It was the elephant in the room. I would have spoken to her honestly about it had she asked but I fear she did not want to make me feel 'confronted' by revisiting the subject and our time together passed without a mention.

Chapter 14 Then and Now: History

Now, after nine months of sobriety I feel fairly secure in my commitment to the long term. Often, the morning after a pleasant evening, I wash the glasses and wonder if in fact I could now be like so many others; have a couple of drinks and accept that's it? Would the lessons I've learned so far keep me mindful that I must not keep on drinking? Sometimes I think yes, I could, but the perceived wisdom is that someone in my situation cannot now magically control their intake. The reasoning is that although our behaviour has changed, the underlying mechanism that makes us drink so differently to others in the first place, remains there, lying dormant but ready to be re-awakened at any time. The triggers to activate those pathways do not go away and if they are allowed the tiniest way back inside the door they will rapidly take over once again, leaving us back where we started. That is a chance I do not wish to take. I'm keeping my belief with the majority and remain cognisant of the fact that after the first or second drink, my mind is no longer purely under my voluntary control and at that stage I cannot do as I may have intended. I am no longer in charge of me.

So while I don't test the theory, it makes me consider what it is within me (and others) that caused my drinking pattern to develop and take hold in such a dysfunctional way?

I wasn't born with it, I don't think and I didn't catch it from another person infected in a similar way.

As with most things it is likely to be a combination of having a genetic predisposition coupled with an environmental trigger. People develop alcohol problems at different times in life, at different rates and of different severity. There is no one size fits all and this is where the difficulty in defining an alcoholic lies.

I've thought about where my trigger point may have been. As a child I was aware of my parents' drinking. I would see them share a bottle of wine on Sundays at dinnertime and remember them having the same joke each week about sharing it equally. Sometimes it meant we could not go anywhere later on as neither of them was fit to drive. I was aware of their nights in when other couples would come around and stay until the early hours. The next day I would be the only one up for hours (it seemed) and would wash all the glasses, empty the ashtrays and tidy up, all in the hope of receiving some praise and thanks from my mum. I was never overtly aware of my parents being drunk (perhaps I did not recognise the signs then) but there is a history of excessive alcohol use on both sides of my family and now I can see how they both drank too much. My father continues to do so, and my mother quietly gave up alcohol completely in her sixth decade, citing general health reasons for doing so. I have attempted to discuss that change of behaviour with her a couple of times since I've stopped drinking but each time the subject is quickly dismissed. She does not talk much about it and I suspect she too, realised her drinking was out of control before stopping it entirely.

I can't remember having my first alcoholic drink but I would have been around sixteen and it would have been martini and lemonade. The first time I remember being drunk was on a holiday, aged seventeen, with a friend. It was not a pleasant experience and I remember not really wanting to drink but felt it was the grown up thing for us to do. I was not drunk often as a teenager and was not particularly attracted to alcohol.

I went to University and at first started drinking lager with lime. I knew my mum often had this and I could bear the taste with enough lime cordial added. I still don't think I drank a lot in my student days. Sure I got drunk perhaps at the weekend, perhaps at the end of term after the exams but in general I had weekend jobs, attended lectures and studied hard. I did not miss alcohol. It was not yet a special feature on my radar.

One New Year some friends introduced me to gin and tonic. A large jug of it had been prepared to share and I was pleased to finally find something appropriately alcoholic that I enjoyed. It became my drink from then on.

Spirits were expensive though and I was a student so still it remained, that alcohol was not a big deal.

As I got older my social life moved from drinking in pubs to dining out in restaurants and having dinner parties at home. I started having wine with meals and managed to find some that I liked the taste of. It was the height of sophistication and maturity, but I still thought wine was overrated and preferred the bottled vodka and bacardi mixes which would later become known as alco-pops.

With time and perseverance however, I grew to enjoy wine and drink more of it. There was a respectability about it. It showed you were mature and sophisticated. It may still do. I loved the weighty feeling of swirling cold white wine in a heavy crystal glass. As a young professional, image was important. I did not go to work drunk. I rarely went to work hungover. My wine intake was restricted by the calories it contained and my desire to remain slim. My longer term intake kept respectable by several years of working many hours whilst simultaneously studying for exams.

After I got married I was definitely drinking more. It wasn't something I noticed or thought much about at the time. It seemed normal. Along with many of our contemporaries we were young, had a double income and no kids. It was usual to drink once or twice in the week and at weekends as a couple. In addition I had regular nights out with friends which were a bit wilder. I don't remember alcohol being a need and I certainly didn't consider it a problem.

The first time I voiced my concerns about drinking was around the age of thirty, before I had children. I noticed I was drinking more. More often, greater amounts each time. I was now using it to unwind and relax as well as to celebrate and socialise. I voiced my concern to my OH once and jokingly said I was worried I was an alcoholic. He laughed and told me not to be daft: it wasn't as if I was emptying a bottle of wine a night or anything, was it?

No, it wasn't. But I was drinking one half of a bottle of wine each night and while I tried to make a bottle continue to last two nights it often became two thirds the first night with only a third left for the next night. It then became reasonable to open another bottle and adjust my own goal posts. Subconsciously, I decided that if my intake increased to a whole bottle per night, then that would be a problem. I also kept telling myself I wasn't quite there yet.

My drinking was then curtailed by pregnancy. I stopped feeling sick about half way through each pregnancy and would then stretch my Governmental guideline of one or two drinks once or twice a week, as far as possible. One drink being counted as one glass of wine. Everyone I knew was doing this at the time. I was still in good company which normalised it to some extent. We laughed at those uptight mums-to-be who were too scared to have any alcohol at all while pregnant, such extreme caution deemed unnecessary and signifying their over-anxiety. Three years later in my mid thirties I had finished having babies and breast feeding. I had finished with post-graduate exams. There was nothing to restrict my drinking now and in fact, there were many factors which encouraged it and made me deserving of it.

We had enough money, we had young children so didn't go out, we were exhausted each evening, we had professional jobs and drinking was the sophisticated way to relax.

This was an inflection point for me, when my drinking really began to escalate. I don't know if I had post-natal depression, but I don't think I did. I fell straight into the trap of trying to be a successful working mother and having it all. A mother who was juggling her work-life balance and crucially, finding and defining, some 'me time'. Me time was wine time. It occurred after the working day was finished, after the chores were done and after the children were asleep. Busy brains needed help to stop whizzing around full of lists of things to do, things to remember and jobs to be done. It was quickly switched off with the first glass of wine and relaxation followed with the second. That wine was required, it was deserved, it was a social norm and not something to be ashamed of. It gave enough brain rest to bring on sleep quickly which would last until the first baby awoke in the night. A spiral quickly developed. More wine, more hangover, more irritable, more harassed, more busy, less able to cope, so more deserving of more wine, leading to more hangover...and so it went on.

Over the next few years my intake of wine increased continually. It was habitual and there was plenty of it. I had more to drink at the weekends then more each night. At some point my desire for wine became a need and as I needed more and more I reached a stage where there was not enough time each day to fit in all the wine that I needed. I did not have enough time to spend all that I needed to on drinking, it being allocated into a neat separate compartment of pure me time.

As the children got older and slightly easier to manage I began to go out more again. Nights out were the ultimate me time. Away from home, away from responsibility, away from any suggestion to call it a day and go to bed. I was free to stay out and drink as much as I wanted. And I did.

I cannot pinpoint when it became a problem or when I became dependent on it but I noticed comments from others which showed they were not as pre-occupied with drinking as I was. I met a friend one Wednesday evening for a chat. She suggested a coffee shop but I preferred the

Tapas bar close by. She had her coffee and looking at my large glass of wine asked me what I was celebrating.

'Nothing,' I said. 'Why?'

'I just wondered what merited a glass of wine mid week?'

By now I drank every night of the week regardless of the day and was surprised that she, clearly, did not.

In realising I was drinking too much I immediately tried to limit it. This had the effect of making it forbidden at times and therefore all the more attractive. It started a want it/shouldn't have it mentality that I spent a lot of time debating over the following years. By the time I began trying to control it, I suspect it was already too late. The alcohol was in control and I was doing whatever I had to, to accommodate it in my life.

I started to plan when I could drink more precisely. If I was working a long shift I would ensure I could drink the night before as well as the night after. I was less inclined to spend time on activities or in places that precluded drinking. I had a lot of it to fit in and I kept on trying to do so for many years before finally giving in and giving up.

Chapter 15 Then and Now: Evenings and Home Life

Then

I used to think I didn't enjoy my home life. It annoyed me, I was dissatisfied by it and couldn't see what was missing. I spent a lot of time 'getting away' and 'getting out' for periods of 'me time'. My role was a chore, a never-ending thankless task that left me exhausted and fed up. No wonder I drank wine. In the evenings I thought I enjoyed a glass of wine, never thinking it had become a need. Never considering it could be compounding my problems rather than providing relief from them. I would drink a bottle of wine whilst flicking randomly through magazines, mumbling about how rubbish they were. The television was rubbish too and I usually fell asleep because it was so boring. Yet I could not be bothered to do anything else. I had lots of ideas, was full of talk about what I could do tomorrow, in the future. Then, when the wine wore off I just could not be bothered with those same things or would plan to do it 'at some point'. Now was never the right time. I had no time. I could hardly keep up with all the things I had to do never mind anything I may want to do.

At weekends I used to think I enjoyed having friends round for dinner. Usually another family would arrive at 3pm and I would convivially open some frivolous pink fizz straight away. It was an excuse to start drinking earlier and to drink more. The idea was that the kids would play together leaving us in peace. I would give them an early tea and keep them pre-occupied with a movie and as many sweets and chocolates as they wished whilst the adults had a sophisticated meal (and more wine of course). I can no longer be bothered to cook for lots of others nor do I particularly want to spend our precious weekend free time with another family.

Now

I enjoy our weekends, pottering around as a family with no great objectives. Maybe a bit of baking, painting a picture or watching television together. I know that wine does not make television any more interesting but staying awake and paying attention does! I feel content with what we have and have stopped striving to do all the hospitality I once did. I convinced myself I enjoyed these afternoons but actually only used them to give an air of respectability to my drinking.

My leisure pursuits have changed significantly. I am much more content at home and now I can be bothered. My children's bedtime is not rushed to get downstairs to pour wine, their evening activities not resented as I'm kept from drinking until later. I no longer resent the school disco and providing lifts to and from it on a Friday night. It is for my family and they are my main concern in life. I enjoy doing jigsaws and have started piano lessons now I have more patience and concentration. I am learning a foreign language at evening classes now that I don't care that it doesn't finish until nine o'clock taking up most of the evening and involves driving and no drinking. There are so many more usable hours in the day now it is no longer truncated at six o'clock when the wine is first opened and brain function starts to decline. I can now do things requiring concentration and mindfulness. I can do on-line banking reliably. I can do internet shopping without scanning my emails the following day to see what I have bought. I can text and email friends sensibly with no need to revisit them the next day, wondering what exactly, I had said. I can concentrate on television and stay awake long enough to watch a film and see the ending. Increasingly I wonder what would be the point of drinking during an evening like this? What would I gain? How could it improve anything?

I am generally a nicer person to be around now. My personality is visible, no longer flattened by a headache, dehydration or exhaustion. I am nicer to my children and nicer to myself too.

Then

I would berate myself continually, nothing ever being good enough. I was too drunk, too hungover, had eaten too much food, had wasted too much time. I felt awful and these thoughts made me feel even worse about myself. I would feel so bad I would deserve a glass of wine that night to cheer myself up. I used to think I was poor at parenting. Continually irritable and not that interested, feeling the children hindered the time available for me and in which to drink. I hated looking after them when hungover. It was probably not very pleasant for them either. I would find it stressful and one of us at least, would always end up in tears. I would be unable to resolve conflict and would think, please, just bring on the wine time and let me escape from this life.

I was completely oblivious to the fact that wine was the cause of all these symptoms. Further, had anyone told me this, I would not have believed it.

Now

I am much kinder to myself. If I overeat I acknowledge it, draw the line and move on thinking I am human after all and we do make mistakes. It's the same if I 'waste' an afternoon snoozing or doing a jigsaw rather than doing something more productive. I can reframe it and think, this is fine, this is my relaxation time, I can enjoy it and need not feel guilty about it. There are no crazy urges to get it all done super-quickly, to then flop with the wine. My life and my mental state seem much more balanced nowadays. I no longer feel chronically depressed. I am calmer, more patient, more interested and better rewarded. I think my children like me more and they know I am here, in mind as well as body, a whole lot more.

Chapter 16 Then and Now:
Christmas and New Year

Then

I remember last Christmas well. I was coming around to the idea that I was going to have to stop drinking at some point, so had to make the most of it while it lasted. I had tried to stop the previous year and found it impossible. Every cafe or bar with fairy lights coming on as it got dark enticed me to enjoy the christmas-y feeling with a lovely drink of something. The parties, the socialising, the visiting, all revolved around drinking and I could not comprehend how life could carry on at this time without drinking alcohol. It seemed by removing alcohol I would ruin the rest of my life and be doomed to spend it miserable and wanting.

So, I drank every day over the Christmas period. It started with the parties in the lead up to Christmas. Each party was a big event where heavy drinking was permitted, if not indeed, expected. Specifics such as cash, house keys, taxis had to be arranged in advance of the time when my brain could no longer function and the next day had to be freed from as much as possible. Sometimes drinking was enjoyable, sometimes it was necessary and sometimes it was for no reason. I recognised having too much of a good thing and its appeal diminishing, but my mind could not fathom having opportunity to drink yet choosing not to do so. So I did, whether I really wanted to or not. Christmas Eve would arrive and I would be exhausted and wrung out after a month of partying. I would be stressed. Sorting out the presents after the kids had gone to bed, knowing this crucial job still had to be done spoiled my enjoyment of drinking wine in the evening beforehand. Once completed it would be late, often midnight, yet with the jobs done I would want to relax with a further glass of wine in peace and quiet. This meant being even later to bed and more hungover early on Christmas morning when I would have to drag myself out of bed as the children rushed, full of life, full of joy and noisy excitement, to open their presents. I would be feeling awful, rebranded for my family as 'tired' and of course guilty that I was not fully sharing their joy.

We usually have house guests over this period and last year was no different. I then drink because I deserve it after all the cooking and clearing away. I need it to deal with the 'stress' and I kid myself that I should offer, and keep offering, alcohol to guests. They don't drink very much but enjoy a small sherry before lunch whilst on holiday. I would join in with that too, generally having more than a thimbleful. I would then bring the wine out at lunchtime and while some would have a small amount while eating, I would continue throughout the meal, into the clearing up period and for most of the afternoon too. I was wary of how my drinking was observed by our guests. I did not want them to think I was drinking too much every day (which I was) and would conceal my glasses within the mess of preparation in the kitchen or beside unwashed glasses. I suspect I did not hide it as well as I thought.

I went to great lengths to make it everywhere we were invited and engineered not to be the one driving. This followed a nonchalant discussion of 'I don't mind, whatever you prefer, I'm happy to drive,' knowing that my OH prefers not to drink at these things as we are still parenting our children, and always prefers to drive. I invited lots of people to our house. Usually families and usually in the afternoon both to enable an earlier start to drinking and because we all had young children. The plan would be for the children to amuse themselves and leave the adults alone, chatting and drinking. I resented the intrusion of the children each time they appeared, interrupting, needing adult input. When their bedtime came I was not particularly interested or patient, wholly focussed on continuing the drinking which, by then, had advanced beyond any boundaries.

Even when there was nothing planned, come early evening I would open another bottle of wine. A couple of times I thought to myself 'Here we go again' when the first sip was a disappointment and merely reminded me of the last time when I'd yet again had too much. But it did not make me stop or take a break. It seemed it was all I knew how to do and there was no realistic alternative.

As the festive period wore on I grew more and more tired, became increasingly bloated and fatter each day as my eating patterns deteriorated and the Christmas cake was still lying around. I gained weight and felt very down about that. I was glad to be working on New Year's Eve. It was a night to drink even more than usual and I was so hungover from the day before that I did not want to drink at all. Working was the only thing that stopped me. I was grumpy and short tempered, annoyed with everything at work and unpleasant to work with, I suspect. I think most of the Christmas 'stress' and 'dramas' I experienced were due to chronic low grade hangover symptoms. Wine, once again the cause of the problems, rather than the solution.

Now

The following Christmas I was nine months free from alcohol and looking forward to the festive period without the worries of enabling my drinking, hiding my drinking or suffering the hangovers

We put up the Christmas tree and it was notably simple and exciting for the children. There did not seem to be any of the stress or drama that I usually associate it with. I didn't mind that the decorations were mis-matched, home-made and not distributed evenly around the tree. My children had been the project managers and I was happy to observe their work. I was productive in December. I was able to make full use of my free time no longer held back by hangovers. I decided not to go to many Christmas parties: not because I couldn't drink but because many had very little appeal remaining when considered without the booze. I went to a few friends' gatherings and enjoyed chatting mindfully and sincerely to others, being a good parent and considerate to my children and leaving after a short but enjoyable time. I love that I can drive everywhere now and doing so is not coupled with frustration at not being able to drink. Looking back, the reason I did not enjoy events I had driven to was due to an overwhelming feeling of frustration at being forced to remain sober, rather than actually choosing to remain sober at a party. Such twisted logic was not uncommon.

We received a crate of fine wine through the post as a Christmas gift. Six red and six white. I was dis-interested and left the box for a couple of days until my husband opened it and perused the selection. Twice he had wine with a meal and each time I observed his drinking behaviour. He poured the glass as the meal was being served, not before. When I looked I saw he had poured a tiny glassful. I would have been horrified if he had poured only that amount for me. We were two-thirds of the way through our meal before he took his first sip. I mean, had he forgotten it was there? He managed to finish it and progressed onto coffee with dessert. As we flopped on the sofa later he poured another, even smaller amount this time. He had a few sips of it over the space of an hour and then left almost an inch in the bottom of the glass: he'd had enough and did not want to finish it. This whole attitude is unfathomable to me. Had I been drinking wine I would have poured large glasses earlier on, taken the bottle to the table for top-ups, shunned the coffee and dessert and continued to drink on the sofa later. Luckily I did not have to do this anymore and I watched him out of interest, rather than with envy or longing for wine of my own.

Unusually, we had no house guests this year and I very much enjoyed our time alone as a family. I was up bright and early on Christmas morning, sharing in the enthusiasm, not resentful at the early hour. The rest of the day was lovely. It did not disintegrate as I got drunk and I did not fall asleep on the sofa after lunch. There was no need to offer wine, open wine, have wine, manage wine. No concern about its continued supply or disposal. I was content to be at home, playing with the children and their new games, preparing simple meals with minimum fuss and no expectation. I did not invite families round on the pretext of catching up but really to excuse another afternoon of drinking. The mere thought of all these visitors makes me feel exhausted and fills me with dread, now that I am content with what I have, what we are. I'm no longer hiding from reality, hiding behind the booze. This year I was not pre-occupied by how I was feeling each day or with what I would be drinking later. I enjoyed watching television without falling asleep on the sofa or appearing rude in front of guests. I relaxed, unwound, felt great and thoroughly enjoyed one of our few remaining Santa years.

Chapter 17 Now

I was worried that as time passed my resolution would wane. However, it seems the longer I have been free from alcohol the less I am affected by rose tinted spectacles. From initially feeling I was missing out, being deprived of a treat, as I approach a year of sobriety I can see more and more clearly the illusion it is. I know and continually remember, that it was never just one or two glasses for me, never could be, and never would be. I couldn't stop once I had started. Wine with lunch either continued or left me spending the afternoon seeking more or impatiently waiting for evening to arrive when I could legitimately continue to drink. Drinking in the afternoon or early evening with friends never ended when they left. I'd continue until it was all gone or I fell asleep. I never knew when enough was enough and I never learnt from my mistakes.

At the beginning all I could think of was what I would be giving up. What I would be depriving myself of. What on earth would I do instead? What would be the point to so many of my outings if not to drink lots of alcohol? I imagined my life would be exactly the same, only minus the alcohol. How would I fill that void? How would I ever feel pleasure or be happy again I wondered.

I never thought I would see how boring many of those things truly were, or that I would choose not to do them anymore, since having loads more ideas and opportunities for more interesting pastimes. I never considered that I would gain so much in so many other areas of my life, areas which I couldn't at that time see, were being restrained by alcohol. Regular drinking takes up a lot of time to the detriment of other pursuits. Hangovers further restrict our abilities to achieve. An attitude of 'there's no time, I can't be bothered, maybe one day'...prevails because right now, I am drinking wine and that is the most important thing.

I still think I do miss out on the pleasure associated with the first and perhaps the second drink. I think of missing champagne on a sunny afternoon or of having wine with a special dinner with my OH. I miss that short period, usually lasting less than an hour, of relaxing into a dreamy state, the conversation flowing, becoming excited from feeling the early effects of alcohol and enjoying the slight blurring of reality as my mind becomes fuzzy. That period of time when alcohol has removed inhibitions but has not yet tipped the balance towards the inebriated, mind altered liability that I am sure to become.

I may miss out on this bewitching hour, but I gain in the other 23 hours of every day.

What I am 'missing out' is basically drug taking. I am not being alarmist or extremist but drinking alcohol is taking a substance to achieve a mind-altered state, to become a different person. As drinking alcohol strengthens its hold, more and more time is spent in this altered version of oneself to the extent that it becomes the norm. This is generally not a nice person. I would regularly become loud, arrogant, boastful, argumentative. I'd talk non-stop. I was always right. My sense of humour would become extreme and my friends would often be the butt of hurtful jokes and home truths. Thinking it was funny I would regularly overstep the mark. Over-sharing, spreading gossip, announcing what I really thought about this and that, not caring who I offended. I was often worried and regretful the next day. Worried I'd gone too far. Wondering if my friends still wanted to be associated with me. What were they saying? Was I that much more drunk than everyone else? Did they remember? Regularly I could not remember the details of many conversations but sometimes I could and I was mortified. At times I could not remember who had been there and who had not and often embarrassed myself as my amnesia became evident some time later.

My behaviour after alcohol seemed so far removed from the normal me. How could it have happened? But happen it did. Time after time after time. My personality when not drunk changed too. Due to the chronic effects of drinking I spent many years being irritable, down, depressed, being in a bad mood, displeased, grumpy. These features became me.

Since giving up alcohol last year I have watched a very different version of me emerge. I am surprised by how my tastes have changed. I am surprised by what brings me happiness, by how I want to spend my time, because for so long, alcohol has dictated these options. I can now choose to do anything I want without a thought as to how alcohol can be fitted in. I am surprised how much happier my baseline mood is. I can engage in small talk, comment on frivolities and interact with shopkeepers now I am not pre-occupied with mere survival, dealing only with essentials until wine-time arrives and I can absolve myself of all thoughts and feelings and escape the hangover from the night before. I can more often see the positives of any situation and am better able to deal with the negatives.

Now I have my life back. It once again belongs to me, is under my control and I can do whatever I choose without my plans being hi-jacked by booze mid-way through. I no longer worry about visiting family, wondering if there will be enough booze, nor of having them visiting my home and observing how much I drink. My mood and motivation are at all time highs. I have lots of time. I have lots of ideas and I have the drive to action them and achieve my goals, no matter how small or insignificant they seem. Now that my mind is not dulled into submission each night I find it works quite well and I am enjoying my new hobbies.

Life in general seems much simpler now. A whole raft of planning, plotting, purchasing, drinking, dealing with and bemoaning have all been removed. Activities can be planned and take place as I wish, if I wish, rather than being orchestrated around boozing opportunities or limited by the anticipated hangover. There seems to be less of a rush about everything. I am no longer looking ahead to the next drinking opportunity, keen to get there, not wanting to be late.

My days are more productive too, but importantly are also more satisfying and enjoyable. There is no hangover of any degree to survive, to battle on with, functioning just enough to meet daily commitments, all the while wishing the time would pass and the hangover be gone.

Compared with those early, difficult days which passed achingly slowly, each day bringing a new challenge, I have come a long way. Keeping each day in the moment I can now accidentally walk into the wine aisle in a store without worrying I will pick up a bottle. I can contemplate forever and the foreverness of what I am doing without panicking at the magnitude of it. I now believe it is possible for me.

I recently considered if I should have one glass of something at one opportunity. Was it really such a big deal? Would the sky suddenly come crashing down? I can predict exactly what would happen. I would have just that one glass that time but would be left back at the table re-starting negotiations over a new round of drinking rules. What about tomorrow? I know if I had wine one night, I would want it the next. What about next week? Very quickly it would all become fair game for a drink at anytime. I know that if I was again given the choice to drink or not, I would always choose to do so. I would never, 'just decide' to do without for a day, a week or whatever. One drink one time would lead to one drink anytime and quickly again onto several drinks anytime and finally to several drinks all the time. I know this because I have practised it repeatedly in recent years, and it works every time.

I truly believe I have now made a positive choice to remove alcohol from my life and in doing so feel that I have finally grown up. I always thought I was the heart and soul of the party but now realise I was simply drunk. I can accept now that by nature I am quiet and shy. I am not comfortable socialising in big groups or with people I don't know well. So I don't do these things anymore. I go out less now I have realised the main attraction for many events I went to was to be able to drink excessively in an environment where it seemed normal. I now do only what I want to do. Sure, sometimes I think I am a bit boring, often preferring a night in with a movie rather than with friends down the pub but I do now, the things I enjoy and I enjoy what I do. I still see friends but tend to meet to walk and talk or go to the cinema or drive to one of their homes.

A romantic dinner for two, or any evening meal out remains a challenge. It is not the same sipping a non-alcoholic drink while perusing the menu. A glass of wine would once stimulate great conversation between OH and I, the type normally lost within the day to day management of child care and chores. I now plan these nights less often, preferring instead to make the meal out an earlier, family affair or as a quick stop on the way to a show or some other form of entertainment. The meal is no longer the main event and it is a small price to pay.

I no longer have true cravings and most of the time I'm pleased I am no longer in the midst of it all but just sometimes, I can still feel wistful when I see a billboard with a tempting glass of wine, or a special offer for a bottle of wine with every order placed or meal purchased. I still, one year on, think this looks nice. I transiently feel I am missing out until I remind myself that it would not be nice. I remember where any amount of wine would take me and leave me and remind myself that I must avoid it. I have to constantly remind myself that there is only a very brief period of enjoyment before it will disintegrate into a horrid phase which will last much longer.

During a night in with the girls I will be watching the others have their first glass of wine and think how nice it looks, how I'd love one too. But I also notice how half an hour later some have barely touched theirs, no one is more than half way through the glass and I know, that I would feel unhappy at this stage. My drinking would be different. I'd be drinking quickly and offering to top everyone up, drinking more than everyone else. This remains very clear to me and I know I never want to go back to that situation. That first cold swirling glass is an illusion for me. It is not what it seems. To me it represents the unleashing of my own inner demon intent on ruining my evening. So I can resist, I do resist, and I continue to resist.

Sometimes I feel I got my just desserts. I could not enjoy wine responsibly so have to go without altogether. I now accept that I am one of a group of people who truly, cannot have one drink. The reason for this is still not obvious. As with most things I think it is a combination of a genetic predisposition coupled with one or more environmental triggers. I do not believe it is an illness but neither is it as simple as having a choice. Alcohol brings with it a compulsion to drink more alcohol. The only choice is choosing to no longer allow alcohol into your life.

And that is the choice I have made.

I hope you enjoyed reading this book.
Share your comments with me at
soberisthenewrachelblack@gmail.com
Or on my blog
soberisthenewrachelblack@blogspot.co

CPSIA information can be obtained
at www.ICGtesting.com
Printed in the USA
FFOW01n2140070216
21255FF